Wardrobes and Rings

Wardrobes and Rings

*Through Lenten Lands
with the Inklings*

Julia Golding
Malcolm Guite
and
Simon Horobin

CANTERBURY
PRESS

© Julia Golding, Malcolm Guite, Simon Horobin 2025
First published in 2025 by the Canterbury Press Norwich
Editorial office
3rd Floor, Invicta House
110 Golden Lane,
London EC1Y 0TG, UK
www.canterburypress.co.uk
Canterbury Press is an imprint of Hymns Ancient & Modern Ltd
(a registered charity)

Hymns Ancient & Modern® is a registered trademark of
Hymns Ancient & Modern Ltd
13A Hellesdon Park Road, Norwich,
Norfolk NR6 5DR, UK

All rights reserved. No part of this publication may be reproduced,
stored in a retrieval system, or transmitted,
in any form or by any means, electronic, mechanical,
photocopying or otherwise, without the prior permission of
the publisher, Canterbury Press.

Julia Golding, Malcolm Guite, and Simon Horobin have asserted their right
under the Copyright, Designs and Patents Act 1988 to be identified as the
Authors of this Work

Unless otherwise noted, Scripture quotations are from New Revised Standard
Version Bible: Anglicized Edition, copyright © 1989, 1995 National Council
of the Churches of Christ in the United States of America. Used by permission.
All rights reserved worldwide.

Bible extracts marked KJV are from the Authorized Version of the Bible (The King
James Bible), the rights in which are vested in the Crown, and are reproduced by
permission of the Crown's Patentee, Cambridge University Press.

Scripture quotations marked (NIV) are taken from the Holy Bible, New International
Version®, NIV®. Copyright © 1973, 1978, 1984, 2011 by Biblica, Inc.™ Used
by permission of Zondervan. All rights reserved worldwide. www.zondervan.com
The "NIV" and "New International Version" are trademarks registered in the
United States Patent and Trademark Office by Biblica, Inc.™

British Library Cataloguing in Publication data
A catalogue record for this book is available
from the British Library

ISBN: 978 1 78622 689 1

EU GPSR Authorised Representative
LOGOS EUROPE, 9 rue Nicolas Poussin, 17000, LA ROCHELLE, France
E-mail: Contact@logoseurope.eu

No part of this book may be used or reproduced in any manner for the purpose of
training artificial intelligence technologies or systems.

Typeset by Regent Typesetting

Contents

About the Authors   viii

Introduction   1

Lent Begins
Ash Wednesday: Turkish Delight   5
Thursday: Galadriel and the Ring   8
Friday: Beowulf and the Dangers of Dragon Treasure   11
Saturday: Eustace and Undragoning   14

Week 1: Nature in the Worlds of Tolkien and C. S. Lewis
Sunday: The Discarded Image   19
Monday: Ransom in 'Space'   22
Tuesday: Spring Comes to Narnia   25
Wednesday: Sam Sees a Star in Mordor   28
Thursday: The Heavens Declare   31
Friday: Eustace and Ramandu   34
Saturday: Mythopoeia, Nature and Stars   37

Week 2: Time and Wizardly Wisdom
Sunday: Legolas and the Nature of Time   43
Monday: Return to Cair Paravel   46

Tuesday: *The Great Divorce* – The Moment to Choose Is Now	49
Wednesday: Charles Williams and the Still Point of the Turning World	52
Thursday: Golden Past	55
Friday: *The Screwtape Letters* – Living in the Present	58
Saturday: Frodo and Gandalf – All We Have to Decide Is …?	61

Week 3: Sub-creation – Creativity and Creation Stories

Sunday: Phantastes and Holiness	67
Monday: Mythopoeia and Sub-creation	70
Tuesday: It All Began with a Picture	73
Wednesday: Tolkien and the Music of Creation	76
Thursday: Creation of Narnia	79
Friday: Daring to 'Incarnate Jesus' – Dorothy L. Sayers	82
Saturday: *A Preface to Paradise Lost* – C. S. Lewis on Milton	85

Week 4: Conversion, Conversation and Fellowship

Sunday: A Momentous Conversation	91
Monday: Mythopoeia: Tolkien's Response	94
Tuesday: Fellowship and Pilgrimage – *The Canterbury Tales* Leads the Way	97
Wednesday: Late or Not-Quite Conversions – Thorin and Gollum	100
Thursday: *The Voyage of the 'Dawn Treader'* – Whose Quest Is It Anyway?	103
Friday: The Inklings and Magdalen	106
Saturday: The Mysterious Great-Great-Grandmother	109

Week 5: Going Through the Wardrobe – The Importance of Story

Sunday: Supposal vs Allegory	115
Monday: Freedom of the Creator – The Nature of Middle-earth	118
Tuesday: Bottled Sunshine – Owen Barfield and the Excavation of Words	121
Wednesday: What is True? Puddleglum and Plato!	124
Thursday: Witches, Woods and Other Creatures	127
Friday: A Spell for the Refreshment of the Spirit	130
Saturday: Through the Wardrobe	133

Holy Week: The Ultimate Sacrifice

Palm Sunday: Ransom and the Future of the Planet	139
Monday: Digory and the Sorrow of Aslan	142
Tuesday: Gandalf Comes Back to Finish a Task	145
Wednesday: Till We Have Faces – What Do You See?	148
Maundy Thursday: Spotlight on Sam 'As One Who Serves'	151
Good Friday: Tolkien, Lewis and the Road to the Cross	154
Holy Saturday: Pause, Poise and Turning Point	157
Easter Sunday: Resurrection of Aslan and the Field of Cormallen	160

Acknowledgements	163
Further Up, and Further In	164
Endnotes	166

About the Authors

Julia Golding is a multi-award-winning novelist, writing for adults, young adults and children. Over a million of her books have been published around the world in over 20 languages. She began her career with *The Diamond of Drury Lane*, which won the Nestlé (Smarties) Gold Award and the Waterstones Children's Book of the Year. She has most recently written a series for children called *Jane Austen Investigates* (SPCK/Lion) and an adult Regency puzzle thriller series for HarperCollins, beginning with *The Persephone Code*. She is also director of the Oxford Centre for Fantasy, a small educational charity established to honour the life, work and faith of the Inklings which has a large online following.

Malcolm Guite is the former Chaplain of Girton College, Cambridge and author of various books on contemporary spirituality. In addition, he is a poet and singer-songwriter and fronts the Cambridge-based band Mystery Train. As a literary critic he has written an acclaimed book on Samuel Taylor Coleridge, *Mariner*, and is an expert on the Inklings, Tolkien and C. S. Lewis. In 2023 he was awarded the Lanfranc Award for Education and Scholarship, for his outstanding multifaceted promotion of the Gospels through poetry, public speaking and scholarship.

Professor **Simon Horobin** is Fellow and Tutor in English at Magdalen College and has lectured and published widely on C. S. Lewis and J. R. R. Tolkien. He holds the position that C. S. Lewis had when he was at the college. He is the author of a number of popular books on the English language published by Oxford University Press; his latest book is *C. S. Lewis's Oxford*, Bodleian Publishing.

Introduction

Between 1930 and 1947, a group of men – academics, editors, doctors, students – met twice weekly at Magdalen College and in the pubs of central Oxford, their regular being the Eagle and Child. Imagine sitting across the bar from them. At first glance there was nothing remarkable about the gathering: most were middle-aged family men, with college teaching responsibilities, talking loudly of the politics of the university, or arguing over topics such as the use of language or eighteenth-century French history. So far, so very Oxford.

Look closer. That slight man with the cockney accent: that's Charles Williams, a poet and novelist with an original mind. That friendly looking chap with glasses and a pipe: that's Owen Barfield, philosopher and writer. Then there's Nevill Coghill, the man whose translation of Chaucer you probably read at school. Two more stand out: that one they call Tollers with his tweed jacket and waistcoat? That is J. R. R. Tolkien, now one of the world's most famous writers, author of *The Hobbit* and *The Lord of the Rings*. And the person calling the meeting to order? That's his friend, C. S. Lewis, known as Jack, author of The Chronicles of Narnia, the science fiction Ransom Trilogy, and many books of Christian apologetics.

These men – roughly 17 in number – were the Inklings: an informal group of like-minded friends who met to share their writing. They had in common that they were men of the academic class, living in Oxford, and all were Christians. In our more diverse age, it is fair to ask: what can they possibly have to teach us?

Describe them another way and they stop looking so uniform

and comfortable. They were veterans of World War One, survivors of the Somme. Orphans. Converts from Atheism. Catholics and Protestants. And in one case, a working-class Londoner with an interest in the occult (Williams). They were friends with Dorothy L. Sayers and T. S. Eliot and formed a literary circle that proved to be at least as influential as the contemporaneous Bloomsbury Group.

How? They were very inspired and very entertaining. They re-made fantasy and revolutionized it. They took their faith seriously – and had fun with it too.

How to use this book

This 40-day book of readings (plus Sundays) picks on themes that emerge from their work, particularly that of Tolkien and Lewis. Arranged in weekly themes to suit the Lenten season, we go from temptation to the cross, via nature, time, creation, conversion and the importance of story. Using the springboard of the Inklings, we include a reflection and a Bible reading to prompt further thought. We believe *Wardrobes and Rings* will have something to say to Christians as well as those who wouldn't give themselves that label. All are welcome aboard to find out what that might be.

Julia, Malcolm and Simon

Lent Begins

Lamppost in an Oxfordshire Garden

ASH WEDNESDAY

Turkish Delight

C. S. Lewis, *The Lion, the Witch and the Wardrobe*

C. S. Lewis wrote one of the most famous scenes of temptation in children's literature. Just say 'Turkish Delight' and many of us immediately remember Edmund's encounter with the White Witch in *The Lion, the Witch and the Wardrobe*. Lucy goes through the wardrobe first and meets a faun. Edmund goes through second and bumps into the villain of the tale: the White Witch on her sleigh. Enticing her new follower, she asks Edmund what he most wants to eat and makes it appear by magic on the snow in a round box tied with a green ribbon. When he opens it, he finds several pounds – not meagre ounces – of Turkish Delight, 'sweet and light to the very centre'. Mouths water even now as we read it.

Why does Edmund give in to the Witch's temptation? Greed? Certainly, but we can pity the boy growing up under wartime sweet rationing. Selfishness? That's also true. He chooses pleasure over duty and responsibility towards his family, entangled with a desire for status and power. As a middle child, Edmund hungers for superiority over his (sometimes) priggish siblings. That prepares the ground for him to welcome the White Witch's offer to make Edmund Prince and then King of Narnia.

Lewis makes clear that Edmund is primed for this mistake by a knot of very human weaknesses, a knot that won't unravel until he meets Aslan. He is proudly self-deluded. 'He did not look either clever or handsome whatever the Queen might say.' And he doesn't question the trustworthiness of the person offering the Turkish Delight. When Lucy meets him and reports the Faun's view of the White Witch, her seizing of the crown and the spell she has placed over all of Narnia, he simply repeats the Witch's claim that fauns are not to be trusted. Edmund is determined to sound more knowledgeable even to the point of ignoring the implications of Lucy's comments.

Lucy is excited at his presence in Narnia and the prospects for them all enjoying and sharing in her discovery. But Edmund can think only in terms of his loss of face: 'He was already more than half on the side of the Witch.' He is also stubborn. He would rather see Lucy suffer, as she continues to insist on the truth of her experiences, than admit that he had been wrong to doubt her. The older children, Peter and Susan, become so concerned about Lucy's apparent delusion that they take it to the professor with whom they are staying. But when they recount the story, he adopts an unexpected perspective:

> 'How do you know,' he asked, 'that your sister's story is not true? ... There are only three possibilities. Either your sister is telling lies, or she is mad, or she is telling the truth. You know she doesn't tell lies and it is obvious that she is not mad. For the moment then and unless any further evidence turns up, we must assume that she is telling the truth.'[1]

Lewis raises the question of who can be trusted to tell the truth: in assessing the validity of a story, we need to focus on the trustworthiness of the speaker. We've already witnessed alternative versions of the reality in Narnia; but the children present the professor with two accounts of the same event with the presumption that only Edmund's version can be true. He challenges this assumption by getting them to reconsider the trustworthiness of the speaker rather than focus on the apparent validity of their account.

Yielding to temptation exacts a cost on Edmund. By giving in to the Witch's temptation, he becomes blind to the goodness and beauty of Narnia. When all four children find their way through the wardrobe and meet the beavers, they are struck by the beauty of the snowy landscape and the homeliness of the beavers' residence. But Edmund cannot enjoy the scene; his vision of Narnia has been poisoned by his encounter with the White Witch.

Reflection

Read Matthew 4.1–11.

What temptations have we given in to that might be blinding us to the goodness and beauty of God's world?

SH

THURSDAY

Galadriel and the Ring

J. R. R. Tolkien, *The Fellowship of the Ring*

If Lent is a time for setting things aside, seeing more clearly, discerning, even as you resist some desires, what it is that you truly desire, then Lothlórien in Middle-earth is a good place to visit during Lent. There is a paradox about the main characters' experience of entering Lothlórien. On the one hand it is an interval of much-needed rest and healing, after the horrors of Moria. It is a place where they can get in touch with and express their grief at the loss of Gandalf. But it is also a place of clarified vision, and for that very reason it is a place and time of testing: testing and clarifying their inner desires – learning, in the light of new insight, to discern the right path. As Galadriel says, 'Seeing is both good and perilous.'

For it is in Lothlórien that each member of the company is held in Galadriel's all-seeing gaze and offered a choice. As Tolkien writes: 'All of them felt they had been offered a choice between a shadow full of fear that lay ahead, and something he greatly desired …' And happily, each of them chooses aright, each is able to continue their quest with a clearer sense of what they are doing and why – even Boromir at this point.

A lesser author would have left it at that: an inviolable and ethereal elf-maiden tests, almost tempts them, so that they can see and deliberately choose the right path. But Tolkien does something far more profound, for in this chapter Galadriel herself is tested and tried, almost unwittingly, by Frodo when he freely offers her the Ring. She sees immediately, more than Frodo does, what is at stake – for her, for the whole quest, and so for the whole of Middle-earth. As Galadriel says to Frodo: 'Wise the Lady Galadriel may be, yet here she has met her match in courtesy. Gently you are revenged for my testing of your heart at our first meeting. You begin to see with a keen eye.' And then she confesses openly to him and to herself that her heart has greatly desired the Ring, and for a moment she allows herself to imagine what it would mean for her to accept his innocent offer. She sees an image of herself as a queen, 'beautiful and terrible as the morning and the night'. But, perhaps because she has confessed the desire and allowed herself to imagine it for a moment, she also sees that it would lead not to joy, but to despair: 'All would love me and despair.' And then, having summoned the vision, she has the grace, the self-sacrifice, to dismiss it, and after a moment of almost unbearable peril and tension she says: 'I pass the test. I will diminish and go into the West and remain Galadriel.'

In Tolkien's vision of things, the greatest as well as the least are subject to temptation; and he knows this of course because he knows that even Christ himself was thus tempted, and that he too passed the test, and he too chose to set aside false glory, to diminish, to continue on his true quest, to empty himself and take the form of a servant, and be obedient even unto death.

And here is another paradox. A little earlier in the chapter Galadriel says, about herself and Celeborn, 'Together we have fought the long defeat.' And for any Christian, a chosen Christian life, refusing the false temptations and blandishments of power, can feel like a long defeat. But in our willingness to fight the long defeat, to make the choices that seem to diminish us, to see evil seem to wax so strong, and goodness seem so weak, to refuse the weapons of the enemy even for what seems a noble fight, that very renunciation is itself the victory, just as the cross is the only way to resurrection.

'What do you wish?' Frodo asks her. 'That what should be, shall be,' she answers.[2] There is no better watchword for a Christian, for it is another way of saying, 'Not my will, but thy will be done.'

LENT BEGINS: THURSDAY

Reflection

Re-read The Lord's Prayer (Matthew 6.9–13). Have there been times in your life when it has been hard for you to say to God, 'Thy will be done'? Have there been times when taking the easy path has turned out to be the wrong turn? What helps you to discern God's will for your life?

MG

FRIDAY

Beowulf and the Dangers of Dragon Treasure

Anon., *Beowulf*; J. R. R. Tolkien, *The Hobbit*;
C. S. Lewis, *The Voyage of the 'Dawn Treader'*

The Anglo-Saxon epic poem *Beowulf* tells of a great hero who, having despatched the night-stalking monster Grendel, and then Grendel's mother, later in life kills a dragon and dies in the process. The story influenced both Tolkien and Lewis, although the two writers used it in different ways. Tolkien disliked the way that critics of the poem tended to read it as an allegory, in which the dragon sitting on its treasure hoard comes to represent the Christian concept of Greed. In *The Hobbit*, Bilbo and the Dwarfs set out to kill the dragon Smaug and return the treasure trove he guards to its rightful owner. In Tolkien's handling of the story, Smaug is much more than an allegorical cipher. Smaug is given a distinct personality of his own – he can be flattered and enjoys the challenge of a riddle. He can be deflected but has sufficient intelligence to deduce that Bilbo's reference to himself as the 'barrel rider' means that he has come from the nearby Lake Town.

In this story there is no straightforward identification of the dragon with the concept of greed. Instead, it is the treasure trove itself that has the power to inspire greed in the hearts of those who allow it. Having successfully reclaimed his family's lost hoard, Thorin finds his character being adversely affected by the long hours he spends in the treasury and his lust for the gold that they have recovered. So, while Thorin's heroic qualities are clearly contrasted with the evil and bloodthirsty dragon, this is not a simple opposition of good versus evil. Thorin is just as susceptible to the power of greed that the treasure can inspire as Smaug himself. In the subsequent negotiations with the Elven King, who considers his people to have a claim to a share in the treasure, Bilbo is hopeful that Thorin will be reasonable and fair. However, Bilbo underestimates the power the gold has over Thorin's heart. Even Bilbo is tempted by the beauty of the Arkenstone and considers retaining it for himself.

A parallel episode appears in the events that take place on Dragon Island in *The Voyage of the 'Dawn Treader'*. But, despite drawing upon similar material to Tolkien, Lewis' method of presenting his dragon is quite different. Having separated himself from his fellow sailors because of an unwillingness to help with the necessary repairs to their ship, Eustace comes across a dragon. However, this dragon does none of the things that we might expect of a dragon: 'It did not sit up and clap its wings, nor did it shoot out a stream of flame from its mouth.' It just falls over and dies. A reader hoping for an exciting encounter between Eustace and the dragon, something like the tense dialogue between Bilbo and Smaug, or the heroic yet fatal combat in *Beowulf*, will be sorely disappointed. However, there is a battle here: it is just not a test of wits, strength or bravery. Instead, just as with Thorin and Bilbo, it is a battle that takes place in Eustace's own heart, provoked by his greed for the treasure. On discovering the hoard, Eustace immediately starts plotting how to steal as much as possible and dreams of the lifestyle it would give him in Narnia or one of its neighbours – countries which he presumes are free from taxation. Because Eustace has not read any books about dragons, he is unaware of the dangers of falling asleep on a dragon's treasure, with 'greedy, dragonish thoughts in his heart'. Where Beowulf's struggle with the dragon is fought with sword and strength, Eustace does battle with the greed that is in his own heart. Where Beowulf conquers the dragon but dies in the process, Eustace loses the fight with his greed and the consequence is that he himself is turned into a dragon.[3]

Reflection

The Old English word for treasure is *maðm* – it is the origin of the word 'mathom', a term used to describe trinkets for which Hobbits have no particular use but are unwilling to throw out. What are the mathoms in our lives for which we have no use, or which are no longer helpful for us? What unhelpful thoughts or desires should we be throwing away?

Read Matthew 6.21:

> Where your treasure is, there will your heart be also.

SH

SATURDAY

Eustace and Undragoning

C. S. Lewis, *The Voyage of the 'Dawn Treader'* and
The Horse and His Boy

It is unexpected to come across in a children's story a profound religious truth that stays with you for the rest of your life, but that is what Eustace's experience of dragonhood is for me. This comes in Chapters 6 and 7 of *The Voyage of the 'Dawn Treader'*. As we read yesterday, skiving off work, Eustace Scrubb (a name he 'almost' deserves, according to C. S. Lewis), heads out alone into the hills rather than spend time with his annoying cousins and the jolly crew of mariners. He arrives in time to see the dying moments of a dragon. In his jubilation that it did not rend him limb from limb but merely collapsed and died, Eustace realizes that the dragon's hoard is now his for the taking. Pondering the possibilities, including whether he must pay tax (he's that kind of boy), he puts on a bracelet and falls asleep on the gold.

Big mistake. Lewis is clear that Eustace hasn't heard the right kind of stories at home that would have warned him against this. What stories does he have in mind? Perhaps he is thinking of Andrew Lang's *The Red Fairy Book* which brought the story of Sigurd from the *Völsunga Saga* to children of his generation. It's the story that Tolkien's mother read to little Ronald, and inspired his Middle-earth dragons. If Eustace had read that story, he would know that to desire a dragon's treasure is to risk turning into a dragon, as happens to Fáfnir.

So far, so familiar. Where Lewis does something wonderful and different is imagining what it takes to 'undragon' someone. In the legends, Fáfnir, Smaug and their ilk have to be despatched by a cunning warrior, wielding a sword or arrow of great power. But we don't want Eustace done away with; we want him saved. First, however, he must learn the lessons of being a dragon. The crew turn out to be very accepting of his unfortunate adventure once they work out his identity. He is shown kindness from an expected direction – Lucy, wielding her magical cordial to ease the pain in his arm – and from an unexpected one. He is befriended by the mouse he had insulted early in the voyage by swinging him by the tail; Reepicheep is 'his most constant comforter', telling him tales to cheer him up.

Eustace changes inside first. He responds well and makes himself useful, ferrying things to the ship and keeping everyone warm at night. 'The pleasure (quite new to him) of being liked and, still more, of liking other people, was what kept Eustace from despair,' writes Lewis. We glimpse Eustace's lonely life before Narnia. He needs this adventure more than the Pevensies who have already learned their lessons on previous visits.

OK, thinks the reader, Eustace has become a better boy: time for him to get the reward of being changed back.

But that isn't how 'undragoning' works, if we understand our dragonskin to be all the things we need forgiven.

The transformation happens in private. Six days later, Eustace returns a boy again. He tells Edmund how a lion came to him and took him to a well to bathe. The lion tells him to undress first but no matter how hard Eustace scratches, however many layers he takes off, he cannot get rid of his dragonskin. The lion says that the answer is to allow him to undress the dragon. And here comes an unsettling image – honest and a bit stomach churning. Eustace compares the lion scratching the skin off to picking 'the scab of a sore place. It hurts like billy-oh but it *is* such fun to see it coming away.' There's a parallel here to the episode in *The Horse and His Boy* where Aravis receives the stripes from the lion's claws to teach her what she did to the slave, drugging her and leaving her to be whipped when she made her escape. This is not a tame lion – sin costs and is painful! The boy Eustace emerges from under the lion's paw, is bathed and dressed, and sent back to the camp, a new creation.

LENT BEGINS: SATURDAY

It is fitting that it is Edmund to whom Eustace tells this tale because, as Edmund says: 'You were only an ass, but I was a traitor.'

Reflection

When we are faced by negative parts of ourselves, bad habits like Eustace's, or nasty behaviour like Edmund's treachery, let's remember Eustace and the undragoning. We cannot get rid of them ourselves but need the lion – Christ – to relieve us of them.

Read 2 Corinthians 5.17.

What skins do you need to shed?

JG

WEEK I

Nature in the Worlds of Tolkien and C. S. Lewis

Bluebells in Wytham Woods where Lewis trained as a young soldier

SUNDAY

The Discarded Image

C. S. Lewis, *The Discarded Image*

When she was eight, my daughter went on a school trip to the London Planetarium. As the projection of the stars opened out above her, the voiceover began to tell the story of the universe. The Big Bang – matter flung out into space forming stars – planets – asteroids. Then came: 'The universe will come to an end—'

My daughter missed the 'in billions, or trillions of years' time' – she was understandably traumatized. Much parental soothing and an attempt to explain scale ensued. She still jokes with a hint of seriousness that this was the most upsetting event of her childhood.

Many of us have a version of this problem, as scientific explanations of the universe make our world so small and the universe so large. We aren't the first to think this. The Psalmist says: 'When I look at your heavens, the work of your fingers, the moon and the stars that you have established; what are human beings that you are mindful of them, mortals that you care for them?' (Psalm 8.3–4).

Douglas Adams put it another way in *The Hitchhiker's Guide to the Galaxy*: 'Space is big. You just won't believe how vastly, hugely, mind-bogglingly big it is. I mean, you may think it's a long way down the road to the chemist's, but that's just peanuts to space.'[4]

If you ever have these moments of mind-boggling terror, C. S. Lewis' *The Discarded Image* might help. The book is based on a series of lectures he gave as a background for students studying medieval literature. He explains the era's scientific model of the universe so that allusions in the writing of the period are accessible to us with our very different ideas of time and space.

He contrasts our modern perspective, which is like 'looking out over a sea that fades away into a mist, or looking about one in a trackless forest', to the medieval model with its planetary spheres: 'To look up at the towering medieval universe is much more like looking at a great building.' The medieval person 'is like a man being conducted through an immense cathedral, not like one lost in a shoreless sea'.[5]

Lewis loves this model of the universe. He calls it 'a supreme medieval work of art', 'the central work ... to which they constantly referred, from which they drew a great deal of their strength'.[6] By contrast, he thinks we are cowed by our modern conception of what's 'out there'.

How does this discarded medieval model help a terrified eight- (or eighty-) year-old? Lewis' prescription for our modern problem comes in his epilogue. After the certainties of the nineteenth century where science claimed to describe what we could all fact-check, we have entered a period where '[a]nything imaginable, even anything that can be manipulated by ordinary (that is, non-mathematical) conceptions, far from being a further truth to which mathematics were the avenue, is a mere analogy, a concession to our weakness.'[7] Physicists struggle to turn what they are investigating with advanced mathematics into words ordinary people can understand, talking about a string theory which has nothing to do with common-or-garden string, or Schrödinger's dead-or-alive cat demonstrating the uncertainty principle in quantum theory. Knowing these limits, writes Lewis, we should respect each scientific model and idolize none, particularly when we realize that 'nature gives most of her evidence in answer to the questions we ask her'. These questions are like a stencil that 'determines how much of the total truth will appear and what pattern it will suggest'.[8] Each model 'reflects the prevalent psychology of an age almost as much as it reflects the state of that age's knowledge.'[9] Putting it another way, as God is out of the picture in scientific circles, our psychology requires a vast, usually meaningless universe, so that's what we model.

But what if you turn the tables and consider a universe created by God, full of his presence and not empty space? Well then, you get something like Lewis' science fiction trilogy. He went back to the medieval model for inspiration, but perhaps a modern interpreter will find a way to do this for a quantum world?

Reflection

Read Psalm 8.

The Psalmist is full of joy at the universe, finding it cause to celebrate that God still cares for us despite this immensity. Where is God in your model of the universe? Can the Psalmist help put him back where he belongs?

JG

MONDAY

Ransom in 'Space'

C. S. Lewis, *Out of the Silent Planet* and 'Bluspels and Flalansferes'

Readers of C. S. Lewis' *The Discarded Image* will know how deeply he felt the differences between an earlier medieval worldview and the modern, purely material or mechanistic model. Our previous reflection on the book introduced us to the idea of different 'models' or images of nature. The earlier 'discarded image' or model of creation is one in which the cosmos is simultaneously material and spiritual: it is alive with joy and praise, full of meaning, a world in which Man's relations with the rest of creation, with the earth and the air, with the elements from which he was formed, with the stars and the planets is mutual and courteous, in which there is a continual connection and correspondence between ourselves and the world we inhabit. By contrast the experience of the modern, post-Cartesian worldview is characterized not by participation, but by alienation, not by meaning but by a sense of meaninglessness, not by communion with the cosmos but by the cold indifference of mere 'matter' and 'empty space'. Pascal in his *Pensées* put that modern experience well when he said: 'The silence of these infinite spaces frightens me.'

But if Lewis expressed this contrast academically in *The Discarded Image*, he puts it much more personally in his novel *Out of the Silent Planet*. There he gives us a vivid picture of a man who has been haunted by the modern conception of space as a vast, meaningless emptiness, and lets us in on the joy of his discovery that perhaps space is not so empty after all. For

Lewis did not accept the modern notion of a meaningless or accidental cosmos. Of course, he accepted modern findings in astronomy and physics about the composition and movement of the heavenly bodies, but not the philosophically naïve modern assumption that they had no meaning or consciousness, which he dismissed as 'the mythology that follows in the wake of science'. So he writes of his hero Ransom's first trip into so-called 'space':

> A nightmare, long engendered in the modern mind by the mythology that follows in the wake of science, was falling off him. He had read of 'Space': at the back of his thinking for years had lurked the dismal fancy of the black, cold vacuity, the utter deadness, which was supposed to separate the worlds.

So Ransom goes on, reflecting on his new experience:

> The very name 'Space' seemed a blasphemous libel for this empyrean ocean of radiance in which they swam. He could not call it 'dead' ... Older thinkers had been wiser when they named it simply the heavens – the heavens which declared the glory.[10]

In that last phrase Lewis was of course alluding to the opening lines of Psalm 19 – 'The heavens declare the glory of God; and the firmament sheweth his handywork' (Psalm 19.1, KJV). Lewis takes us in a single paragraph from Pascal's fear of empty space to the Psalmist's certainty that all these beautiful stars, spoken into being by the Word himself, are themselves full of meaning; they are speaking to us, they are declaring God's glory.

As it happens science itself is catching up with Lewis and is now telling us that there is far more in the cosmos than we can ever perceive, that there is dark matter and dark energy, not dark because they are in any sense sinister but because they are occluded from us. Science itself, of course, is properly speaking only competent to tell us what things are, and where they are; it does not even address the question of what they *mean*. Reason, particularly analytic reason, can only take us so far. As

Lewis was later to say in his strangely titled essay 'Bluspels and Flalansferes', we need another organ of knowledge in addition to Reason. 'Reason', he writes, 'is the natural organ of truth, but Imagination is the organ of meaning.'[11] And this of course is why he wrote works of imagination as well as works of theology and literary criticism, and it is why, in the course of this Lent book, as we seek to connect with the meaning that gives purpose and coherence to our lives, we turn to the imaginative works of the Inklings.

Reflection

Read Genesis 1.1–28, and John 1.1–14.

What difference does it make to the way you see the world if you think that everything you see is made in and through Logos, the Word, or mind of God?

MG

TUESDAY

Spring Comes to Narnia

C. S. Lewis, *The Lion, the Witch and the Wardrobe*

Lent, or Lenten, gets its name from an old word meaning 'lengthen' and refers to the time of year when the days get longer. And so, in the northern hemisphere, the Christian season associated with abstention and privation is closely linked to the season in which the world begins to warm and nature stirs with new life. This is beautifully evoked in *The Lion, the Witch and the Wardrobe* in the evocative description of Aslan's arrival bringing about the weakening of the Witch's spell that has trapped Narnia in an eternal winter.

The first signs of this are the trees throwing off their snowy robes and patches of green grass appearing in the fields. The mist that has covered the land is burnt off by shafts of golden sunlight, leaving a striking blue sky. This is followed by the sudden appearance of colourful flowers – celandines and snowdrops – and the noise of gurgling water as the rivers and streams begin to unfreeze. Soon after the children hear the chattering and chirruping of birds so that within moments the whole wood is ringing with birdsong. The light breeze wafts delicious scents into the children's nostrils.

While it takes months for the English countryside to shake off the cold, grey gloom of winter and welcome in the spring, in Narnia the whole process takes a matter of hours. For the children and the beavers, who have endured the lengthy winter brought about by the Witch's spell, the change is an assault on the senses. As they walk, they drift in a delicious dream, drinking in the sounds, smells and vibrant colours and revelling in the feeling of the hot sun on their faces. For the Witch and the Dwarf who drives her sleigh, the coming of spring is evidence of the loosening of her grip over Narnia and the weakening of her powers. There are practical problems too, since a sleigh needs snow to run smoothly. No matter how hard the Dwarf whips the poor reindeer, the sledge continues to slow down, as the snow gives way to slush and then disappears entirely. For Edmund, the realization that the frost is thawing causes his heart to jump for joy, though he hardly knows why.

While Lent is a season in which we prepare for Easter, it is also the time to rejoice in the beauty of nature and God's creation. The Witch's eternal winter disrupts the cycle of the seasons, depriving Narnia's residents of the consolations offered by the beauty of nature. But, while spring brings joy to the senses of the children and the Narnians, with the prospect of a Narnia free from the curse of the Witch, the Witch cannot appreciate its beauty.

Reflection

How often do you take time to rejoice in the green returning to the trees, the beautiful colours of the delicate spring flowers that push their heads out of the ground and drink in their fragrant scents? How often do you stop to listen to the birdsong that fills our countryside, and even our towns and cities, as resident species and returning migrants – their presence a further reminder of the turning of the seasons – begin calling to their mates and marking out their territories? We are so used to walking with headphones pressed into our ears, listening to a favourite album, audiobook or podcast, that social media influencers have coined the term 'silent walking' to describe going for a walk without any kind of audio distraction. This Lent, why not leave your phone at home and go out in the countryside and appreciate the sights, sounds and smells of spring, and remember that it is a sign of Aslan's return and his defeat of the White Witch and the end of her reign over Narnia.

SPRING COMES TO NARNIA

Read Song of Solomon 2.11–13:

> [F]or now, the winter is past,
>   the rain is over and gone.
> The flowers appear on the earth;
>   the time of singing has come,
> and the voice of the turtle-dove
>   is heard in our land.
> The fig tree puts forth its figs,
>   and the vines are in blossom;
>   they give forth fragrance.

SH

WEDNESDAY

Sam Sees a Star in Mordor

J. R. R. Tolkien, *The Return of the King*;
Dante, *The Divine Comedy*;
Shakespeare, *The Merchant of Venice*

One of the most moving moments in *The Lord of the Rings* comes towards the end. Sam and Frodo are deep into the darkness, fear, and barren horror of Mordor, close to despair, when suddenly Sam looks up and sees a star still shining through the gloom:

> The beauty of it smote his heart, as he looked up out of the forsaken land, and hope returned to him. For like a shaft, clear and cold, the thought pierced him that in the end the Shadow was only a small and passing thing: there was light and high beauty for ever beyond its reach.[12]

We cannot help but be moved by that, because the star is not a random symbol dreamt up by Tolkien and imposed on us in some artificial allegorical way. Indeed Tolkien himself said that he 'cordially disliked allegory'. This passage moves us because we have all looked up and seen the stars ourselves. And not simply seen them but in some sense understood them. The Psalmist was right not only poetically but actually when he said, 'The heavens declare the glory of God; and the firmament sheweth his handywork' (Psalm 19.1, KJV).

Tolkien himself was deeply immersed in the long tradition in which writers and poets have felt the stars to be a sign of hope in darkness, sensing on seeing them that 'there was light and high beauty' forever beyond the reach of the shadow. Dante chose to end each of the three great books of his *Divine Comedy* with the word *stelle* meaning 'stars'. Indeed the final lines of Dante's *Inferno* may well have been consciously or subconsciously in Tolkien's mind when he came to write this great passage. For the two companions Frodo and Sam are in very much the same place as those other two companions, Dante and Virgil, as they make their way through, and eventually out of, hell:

> So now we entered on that hidden path,
> My lord and I, to move once more towards
> A shining world. We did not care to rest.
> We climbed, he going first and I behind,
> Until through some small aperture I saw
> The lovely things the skies above us bear.
> Now we came out and once more saw the stars.[13]

Those stars are not a mere glimmer of light in darkness, they are signs of eternal beauty and order, harbingers of heaven itself.

But Tolkien would not have needed to look to the great Italian poet for inspiration, for there is as it were a star-lit pattern woven into the great works of English literature, in which a glimpse of the star-lit heaven gives us a sense that, somewhere beyond the darkness and confusion of our own struggles, there is an eternal beauty to which we can aspire and which can guide us. Tolkien would have known the beautiful passage in *The Merchant of Venice*:

> Look how the floor of heaven
> Is thick inlaid with patines of bright gold:
> There's not the smallest orb which thou behold'st
> But in his motion like an angel sings,
> Still quiring to the young-eyed cherubins;
> Such harmony is in immortal souls;
> But whilst this muddy vesture of decay
> Doth grossly close in it, we cannot hear it.[14]

The stars are here glimpsed in contrast with our own 'muddy vesture of decay', which itself would be a pretty good description of the state Sam and Frodo were in when he glimpsed the star.

Though in one sense *The Lord of The Rings* is an utterly unique work, *sui generis*, in another it is part of a long tradition of stories that kindle hope in darkness. The Bible, Dante and Shakespeare were all forming and focusing Tolkien's imagination, as Tolkien in his turn forms and focuses ours.

And when we ourselves step outside and look up at the stars, we are part of that tradition too and all its insights are available to us.

Reflection

Read Hebrews 12.1–3.

Jesus was able to endure the cross 'for the sake of the joy that was set before him'. What are the visions and signs of joy that help you not to lose heart in the present struggles?

MG

THURSDAY

The Heavens Declare

John Milton, 'Comus';
Samuel Taylor Coleridge, 'Frost at Midnight';
Malcolm Guite, *David's Crown*, 'Sonnet XIX'

Several of our reflections over the last few days have alluded to Psalm 19 with its wonderful opening line: 'The heavens declare the glory of God; and the firmament sheweth his handywork.' It was C. S. Lewis' favourite psalm, indeed he said it was 'the greatest poem in the Psalter and one of the greatest lyrics in the world'. Michael Ward has shown in his brilliant book *Planet Narnia* how deeply Lewis responded both to the beauty of the stars and planets and also to the wonderful penumbra of poetry, song and story that has been associated in all ages and cultures with their radiance, their dance through the skies, and the sense they give us of an eternal splendour above, in Milton's phrase, 'the smoke and stir of this dim spot / Which men call earth' ('Comus', lines 5–6). It is in some respects a seminal and prophetic psalm for our own age. As we have seen in previous reflections, our modern age has, in Lewis' phrase, been haunted by '[a] nightmare, long engendered in the modern mind by the mythology that follows in the wake of science'. That nightmare is the idea that 'space' is no more than 'the black, cold vacuity, the utter deadness, which was supposed to separate the worlds'. And behind that nightmare lies the modern assumption that creation is not really 'creation' at all but a random concatenation of matter and energy which has no meaning. But once we consider the cosmos as *creation*, then we perceive in it the artistry, beauty and purpose which goes with intentional creation. Then we can see the analogy between our own smaller works of 'sub-creation', as Tolkien called it, our poems and stories, and the great poem, the great story in which we find ourselves.

A poet who thought about this deeply, in the midst of the Enlightenment thinking that gave birth to the bleak modern view, was Samuel Taylor Coleridge. He resisted the mechanistic, Newtonian model of nature as being like a piece of clockwork, a machine, and wondered if it wasn't more like an utterance, a poem. In the poem 'Frost at Midnight' he imagined his infant son Hartley growing up amid the sights and sounds of nature and wrote:

> ... so shalt thou see and hear
> The lovely shapes and sounds intelligible
> Of that eternal language, which thy God
> Utters, who from eternity doth teach
> Himself in all, and all things in himself.
> Great universal Teacher! he shall mould
> Thy spirit, and by giving make it ask. (lines 58–64)

That insight tallies exactly with the meaning of Psalm 19, that the heavens are not simply existing, they are also telling us something, they are 'declaring the glory of God'.

Psalm 19 is also a favourite of mine and in my book *David's Crown*, a sequence of poems written in response to each of the psalms, I approached it with some trepidation because it meant so much to me. In the end, however, I found in it an invitation just to enjoy and celebrate beauty in verse.

In this poem the phrase 'the complete consort dancing', the idea that the stars are themselves words in God's poem, is drawn from Coleridge's insight that all the appearances of nature are themselves 'the lovely shapes and sounds intelligible / Of that eternal language, which thy God / Utters'.

XIX *Caeli enarrant*

In that still place where earth and heaven meet
Under mysterious starlight, raise your head
And gaze up at their glory: 'the complete

Consort dancing' as one poet said
Of his own words. But these are all God's words:
A shining poem, waiting to be read

Afresh in every heart. Now look towards
The bright'ning east, and see the splendid sun
Rise and rejoice, the icon of his lord's

True light. Be joyful with him, watch him run
His course, receive the gift and treasure of his light
Pouring like honeyed gold till day is done,

As sweet and strong as all God's laws, as right
As all his judgements and as clean and pure,
All given for your growth, and your delight!

Reflection

Read Psalm 19 and then read my poem alongside it.

What does a starlit night mean to you? Can you remember particular times in your life when the beauty of nature has blessed or healed you?

MG

FRIDAY

Eustace and Ramandu

C. S. Lewis, *The Voyage of the 'Dawn Treader'*,
The Magician's Nephew and *The Discarded Image*

As the Pevensie children explore the fantastical world of Narnia, they are frequently struck by the beauty of the sky and its stars. As they sail to the Utter East in *The Voyage of the 'Dawn Treader'*, Lucy notices how new constellations emerge each night – ones that had never been seen by any living being before that moment. But just as new stars appear in Narnia, so can stars become old and need to be retired in order that they might be restored to their former youth, at which point they can return to rejoin the great dance in the sky.

Lewis' vision of the heavens in Narnia is influenced by the medieval understanding of the cosmos. In the account of creation in *The Magician's Nephew*, the stars appear suddenly in the dark sky – at one moment there was only blackness and the next moment thousands of points of light appear: 'single stars, constellations, and planets, brighter and bigger than any in our world'.[15] The stars' appearance coincides with the sound of beautiful singing, giving the impression that it was the stars themselves that were making the music.

Lewis was greatly attracted by the medieval view of the cosmos, which he described in detail in his book *The Discarded Image*, based upon his university lectures. As we read earlier, in the book he encourages his readers to go outside at night and look up at the sky. Where we now consider ourselves to be looking out into a dark void, medieval people would have felt as if they were looking up into a vast, lighted edifice, like a cathedral.

According to this worldview, the stars and planets circled the earth, producing a beautiful music known as the 'music of the spheres'. Because of the fall, the earth has been cut off from the rest of the cosmos and no longer participates in the music of the spheres. For this reason it is known in his Ransom Trilogy to the inhabitants of Malacandra (Mars) as Thulcandra (the Silent Planet).

In the following chapter of *Voyage*, the children meet Ramandu, a star at rest. Having become old and decrepit, Ramandu was taken to an island where he is fed a fire-berry by a bird, sourced from the valleys in the sun, and each fire-berry makes him a little bit younger. When he has finally become like a new-born child, he will rise again and return to the skies. The astonishment generated by the creation of the stars, witnessed by Digory and Polly, and the discovery of new constellations and meeting a retired star which provoke a wonder in Edmund and Lucy, is entirely lacking in Eustace, with his purely materialistic understanding of the world.

When Ramandu explains that he is a star at rest, Eustace responds by contrasting this with his own world, in which a star is 'a huge ball of flaming gas'. 'Even in your world, my son, that is not what a star is but only what it is made of,' Ramandu retorts.[16] Eustace, we are told at the beginning of the story, had wasted his time at school reading only books of information about exports and imports, so it is no surprise that he can only comprehend a purely materialist definition. If he'd only read more fairy stories, he might have been able to grasp this reality, as well as being better prepared for his adventure on Dragon Island. Eustace needs to take Lewis' advice and look up at the night sky through the eyes of medieval man, marvelling at the fixed stars and beyond them the Primum Mobile, or 'First Mover', which conveys movement to all the other planets and stars, and who himself is moved through a desire for God. He needs to learn from Ransom's experience when finding himself abducted and transported to Mars on a spaceship. Through this experience, Ransom comes to view space not as a 'black, cold vacuity', but rather as an 'empyrean ocean of radiance', which would be more appropriately termed 'the heavens'.[17]

Reflection

Read Job 38.4–7 out aloud and celebrate!

> Where were you when I laid the earth's foundation?
> Tell me, if you understand.
> Who marked off its dimensions? Surely you know!
> Who stretched a measuring line across it?
> On what were its footings set,
> or who laid its cornerstone –
> while the morning stars sang together
> and all the angels shouted for joy?

SH

SATURDAY

Mythopoeia, Nature and Stars

J. R. R. Tolkien, 'Mythopoeia', *The Silmarillion*
and *The Return of the King*

Why did Jesus go into the wilderness for 40 days?

You likely have several answers to do with the temptations, and prayerful preparation, but perhaps there is another consideration? Jesus wanted to be alone in nature. Perhaps he knew what was coming when he couldn't get five minutes peace? Even when he got on a boat to escape, the people would chase him around the Sea of Galilee and still be there with their needs and their questions when he landed. This was his last chance to be on his own to contemplate the heavens, the desert, and the magnificence of creation.

And how would he have voiced what he saw? It is – naturally enough – hard to get inside Jesus' mind, but we know what books he had been reading that would have given him a language to describe his world. Jesus' prayer book, the Psalms, would have provided words to marvel and praise creation. Or perhaps he might have quoted Job, where God answers Job out of the whirlwind. Maybe Jesus recited from Genesis 1? *In the beginning ...* How marvellous would that be, to hear the Word who was with God at the beginning, speaking those words as he looked up at the moon and the stars, or to give thanks for the sun as it flushed the sky pink at dawn, or when he saw a green shoot thrusting out of a crack in a rock.

Having the poets and mythmakers go before us to give us a language for what we see is like putting on the very best pair of sight-correcting glasses. We see more, thanks to the inspiration of those who have seen it first. If you've been through an eye test, you will recall the lenses that are dropped into the heavy frame the optician asks you to wear. Is number one clearer, or number two? Can you read the bottom line? Are the dots clearer on the red or the green? You can think of the box of world myths as a set of lenses. Some lenses might be blurry, but some are crystal clear.

In 'Mythopoeia', the poem Tolkien sent Lewis after their discussion in 1931 of True Myth and belief, he drops the myth lens into the spectacles and writes: 'He sees no stars who does not see them first / of living silver made'. Stars 'burst / to flame like flowers beneath an ancient song', the echo of the music staying with the beholder long after the tune has ended. This is compared to the person of impoverished vision that allows no poetry, no sight-enriching lens, where 'a star's a star, some matter in a ball', a forerunner of the Eustace we met yesterday.[18] Tolkien says acerbically that he does not walk with this kind of 'progressive apes' whose ways lead to the abyss; he will stick with his mythopoeic mirror which contains 'the likeness of the True'.

Of course, in a fantasy, you can make a star into something outside the realms of physics. In Middle-earth, the stars are put in the sky by Elbereth, one of the Valar, or gods. They are a symbol of beauty untouched by evil. One of them is also a person, Elrond's dad in fact! Eärendil goes on a quest to the Blessed Realms of the West to appeal for help to defeat Melkor, the original Dark Lord. He takes with him a Silmaril, or elven jewel, filled with the light from the first days of creation, and goes where no mortal should go. His bravery is rewarded and the Valar intervene to bind Melkor, but it is at the price of Eärendil not being allowed to return to Middle-earth. Instead, he becomes the evening star with the Silmaril bound to his breast, sailing in his ship, Vingilot, across the heavens. It is the kind of story familiar from Greek myth, like those of Perseus and Orion, whom we still trace in the sky at night.

This isn't meant to denigrate the scientific discoveries of what a star is through a scientific lens; it is about a different way of seeing a fragment of the truth. Seen through a mythic lens stars remind us of beauty and of courage. Nothing we can do can reach or mar them – they are truly beyond our power.

Reflection

Read Genesis 1.26–28.

God created humankind to be stewards of his creation. We can't leave this week without acknowledging that we aren't very good at fulfilling that role. Human activity is putting the balance of nature at risk, something Tolkien particularly hated and portrayed in the 'Scouring the Shire' chapter at the end of *The Return of the King*. What can you do to defend the earth from those who would scour it?

JG

WEEK 2

Time and Wizardly Wisdom

The Radcliffe Camera, part of the Bodleian Library,
home of wizardly wisdom?

SUNDAY

Legolas and the Nature of Time

Lewis Carroll, *Alice's Adventures in Wonderland*;
J. R. R. Tolkien, *The Nature of Middle-earth* and
The Fellowship of the Ring

Many of us this week will declare 'I'm late! I'm late for a very important date!' as we rush to pick up children from school, hurry to a meeting, or hoof it to a hospital appointment. We are quoting, not an Inkling, but their Oxford-based predecessor Lewis Carroll and his in-a-hurry White Rabbit.

In fact, Carroll's rabbit (rather than the Disney version) says: 'Oh dear! I shall be too late!'[19] Too late for what? The rabbit is worried about arriving in time for his duties with the irascible Queen of Hearts, so it is understandable that he feels under pressure. However, the White Rabbit represents us as we run through life, juggling multiple responsibilities and always feeling 'too late'. Like a bad dream, we run, but we can never catch up.

In contrast to a 'White Rabbit' existence, consider that of Legolas the Elf. In Middle-earth, Tolkien invented races of people who are almost immortal. That gave him an intriguing challenge: to imagine time for the different perspectives of the long- and short-lived. In *The Nature of Middle-earth*, you can follow him meditating on this as he draws up actuarial tables of elven life experiences in human years. That leads to the rather disconcerting guesstimate that pregnancy lasts nine years. I do hope Elves don't suffer from morning sickness.

In *The Fellowship of the Ring*, Legolas beautifully describes the long and the short view. The Fellowship spend weeks in Lothlórien, healing after the loss of Gandalf in Moria, before they must return to their quest. Setting out in boats given to them by the Elves of that land, the company float down the Silverlode to join the Great River. The rivers become an image of time. For Frodo, it feels as if the time spent in Lothlórien was in the past and they only rejoined the ordinary time once swept into the Great River. This prompts Legolas to give his first long speech to a Hobbit – and it is worth waiting for. Time 'does not tarry ever', he tells Frodo, 'but change and growth is not in all things and places alike'. He goes on to explain how, for his folk, the world 'moves both very swift and very slow'. It moves swiftly because everything around them rushes by, but also slowly as they do not count the years for themselves. 'The passing seasons are but ripples ever repeated in the long long stream.' But he goes on to say that even for the Elves, 'all things must wear to an end at last'.[20]

Legolas is one of the oldest in the Fellowship, but his age is dwarfed (if Gimli will forgive the pun) by the lady they just left. Galadriel is one of the original generation of Elves born in the West and is over 8,000 years old. Then there is Treebeard whom Pippin and Merry meet later. Gandalf calls him the eldest and chief of the Ents, 'and when you speak with him you will hear the speech of the oldest of all living things'.[21] Famously the language of the Ents 'takes a very long time to say anything in it, because [the Ents] do not say anything in it, unless it is worth taking a long time to say'.[22] Eldest is Tom Bombadil, who rescues the Hobbits early on in their adventure. Elrond calls him Iarwain Ben-adar, 'oldest and fatherless', and Glorfindel, one of the Elf lords, predicts Bombadil will fall 'Last as he was First'.[23]

But before you conclude that Tolkien was in favour of stopping or turning back time, he criticizes the Elves as 'embalmers', who try to stop the growth of Middle-earth and are overburdened with 'sadness and nostalgic regret'.[24] So perhaps the lesson is that we shouldn't embalm by clinging on to something that has passed, nor should we 'be hasty' and rush through life like the White Rabbit. A healthy attitude to time rests somewhere between.

Reflection

When are you a White Rabbit and when an Elf?

Read 2 Peter 3.8–9.

For the Lord 'one day is like a thousand years, and a thousand years are like one day'. Hold that thought!

JG

MONDAY

Return to Cair Paravel

C. S. Lewis, *Prince Caspian*

The second Narnia story, *Prince Caspian*, tells of the children's return to Narnia. It opens with them sitting at a railway station awaiting the trains that will take them back to their boarding schools for the start of term, when suddenly they are transported instead back to Narnia. As they take stock of their surroundings and try to make sense of what has happened, they stumble across some apple trees and the ancient ruins of what was once a castle. It takes them some time to recognize the ruins as the remains of their own Cair Paravel, since only a year has passed since they left Narnia and the ruinous state of the castle implies a much longer time. As the realization begins to dawn on the children, they feel a sense of nostalgia for their past life as kings and queens of Narnia, recalling the happy times they spent with the fauns, giants and mer-people.

This description of the destruction of Cair Paravel and its reduction to rubble provides an effective contrast with the constancy of the stalwart badgers that the children meet later. As the badger Trufflehunter retorts to Nikabrik: 'You Dwarfs are as forgetful and changeable as the Humans themselves. I'm a beast, I am, and a Badger what's more. We don't change. We hold on.' But more important than their staying power are the badgers' memories and their faith in the promise that there is a true king of Narnia who will return to restore it to its former glory. Trumpkin scornfully dismisses such fabulous old tales about King Peter reigning at Cair Paravel, but Trufflehunter doubles down in his certainty that such stories are true: 'I believe in the High King Peter and the rest that reigned at Cair Paravel, as firmly as I believe in Aslan himself.' This cuts no ice with Trumpkin, who simply mocks the idea that anyone nowadays should believe in such a figure. But Prince Caspian himself comes to Trufflehunter's defence, asserting his own belief in Aslan and pointing out that many humans don't believe in Dwarfs and talking animals, 'Yet there you are.'[25]

Here Lewis is asserting the importance of stories for communicating truths and the danger of dismissing them as feigned nonsense. The 1,300 years that have passed since the reign of the Pevensie children means that they have once again taken on a mythical status among the inhabitants of Old Narnia. The beasts have no evidence of their existence, nor that of Aslan, but nevertheless they have faithfully passed on the stories through the generations and held fast to the truths they communicate. Trufflehunter's assertion of his faith is a kind of creed, which summarizes the key tenets of his faith: 'I believe in the High King Peter and the rest that reigned at Cair Paravel, as firmly as I believe in Aslan himself.' We might compare this statement of belief with the Apostles' Creed and its opening statement, 'I believe in God the Father almighty, maker of heaven and earth.'

The tendency for such stories to be dismissed as merely myths or fairy stories, recounting fabulous adventures of fantastical beasts like human beings, is an important reminder of the value of the stories of the Bible for continuing to transmit the Christian faith to new generations in a society where such tales are frequently dismissed. It's not just the stories that are important in passing on the Christian faith, it is also the people. The passage we have considered provides an effective contrast between the transitoriness of humans, and the edifices that they build, and the steadfastness of the badgers. Where human rulers come and go, badgers remain. Where humans build impressive castles made of stone, these tumble down and become ruins. And yet the networks of underground tunnels built by the badgers continue to be occupied centuries later. As Trufflehunter says, badgers are not like humans: 'We don't change. We hold on.'

Reflection

Are we guilty of being changeable in our faith, failing to hold on to the truths that led us to faith in the first place? Can we learn from the steadfast badgers, clinging on to those truths even when the world around us rejects them?

Read John 20.29 (NIV):

> Then Jesus told him, 'Because you have seen me, you have believed; blessed are those who have not seen and yet have believed.'

SH

TUESDAY

The Great Divorce – The Moment to Choose Is Now

C. S. Lewis, *The Great Divorce*

One of the most striking episodes in Lewis' allegorical work *The Great Divorce* is the encounter with the man who has a lizard on his shoulder. It comes in Chapter 11, a chapter which juxtaposes two kinds of love: one, to our eyes, seemingly higher, and the other seemingly lower. The first is a mother's love for her son, and the other is a man's lust, his carnal desire.

In both cases the crucial question is, can we put God first? Can we give back to him all our earthly wishes and longings? Are we ready to lose them for his sake, but also, because of that willingness to let go, open to receiving them back, purged and clarified, dead and risen, obedient now to the great Love of God himself? In that Love all our lesser loves can thrive and be renewed; but without it, all our loves will turn greedy, sour, self-centred, even predatory.

The biblical watchword for this whole chapter is '[S]eek ye *first* the kingdom of God ... and all these things shall be added unto you' (Matthew 6.33, KJV, my italics). The mother has allowed mother love to become possessive, controlling, monomaniac. It feeds her need, it has no properly disinterested love or care for her son's real flourishing and independence. Indeed, it becomes clear that she would rather bring him back down to hell with her than love him in heaven, on heaven's terms.

Then, by contrast Lewis shows us the adventure of the man with the lizard on his shoulder. The lizard clearly represents lust,

WEEK 2: TUESDAY

an obsessive appetite that is controlling the man, literally riding on him, when he should be riding and controlling it. The man himself knows this is a problem and is genuinely struggling with it. Indeed the first thing we hear him say to the lizard is, 'Shut up I tell you!' as the lizard constantly whispers and insinuates in his ear. The man finds his lizard 'damned embarrassing' and says to the angel whom he encounters: 'Of course his stuff won't do here. I realize that. But he won't stop. I'll just have to go home.' And then the man is offered by the angel a moment of real choice:

> 'Would you like me to make him quiet?'
> 'Of course I would.'
> 'Then I will kill him.'

This is indeed the moment of crisis, the moment of final choice. The man shies away, tries to back out of it, or at least put it off: 'Well there's time to discuss that later'; but the angel replies, 'There is no Time' – which is strictly speaking true for the man has left the realm of time and is standing on the threshold of eternity. 'Some other day perhaps,' says the man. 'There is no other day,' says the angel, 'all days are present now'; and again, even more tellingly: 'This moment contains all moments.'

Lewis is here riffing on a beautiful discussion of Time and Eternity in Boethius' *Consolation of Philosophy*, in which Boethius memorably describes eternity as a *nunc stans*, an eternal, ever-present 'now' with no before or after. Here there can be no procrastination. The man's *kairos*, the hour of his visitation, has come, he must make his choice. 'Damn and blast you ... get it over,' he says, but follows it up with the best and only prayer for such a moment: 'God help me. God help me.'

The angel seizes the lizard and flings it to the ground where its back is broken. But then Lewis shows us something wonderful and unexpected, a 'eucatastrophe', as Tolkien would say. After this moment of complete submission to God's will both the man and the lizard are transformed. The man becomes fully human, no longer a ghost, and the lizard which had ridden him becomes a great stallion, which he can ride and which will bear him into the highest heaven. Lewis (the narrator) is astonished, but George MacDonald, the Victorian writer and his guide in the adventure, reveals the meaning of what he has seen: 'Nothing, not even the best and noblest, can go on as it is. Nothing, not even the lowest and most bestial, will not be raised again if it submits to death.'

Reflection

Read Matthew 16.24–27.

Are there parts of your life, of your hopes and desires, that you need to let go, to give again into God's hands? How might they be transformed when he gives them back to you?

MG

WEDNESDAY

Charles Williams and the Still Point of the Turning World

Charles Williams, *The Greater Trumps*;
T. S. Eliot, 'Burnt Norton';
W. B. Yeats, 'The Second Coming'

Have you ever met someone who is so different from others that you feel you are in the presence of an original? That was the effect of meeting the oddest of the Inklings, Charles Williams. A Londoner, largely self-taught, with a strong cockney accent, he is hard to categorize. He was known as a poet and mentioned alongside T. S. Eliot. He was a publisher, playwright, and novelist. He was also a wizard of sorts. This is the man who impressed both Lewis and Tolkien, so much so that they invited him to participate in the Inklings and arranged for him to deliver a lecture series at Oxford University. They admired him, even though he came between them, absorbing C. S. Lewis' attention in the way Tolkien once had.

But you are probably wondering about the wizard. Williams belonged to the Fellowship of the Rosy Cross and practised magic rituals. As a member of the Rosy Cross, Williams was fascinated by 'co-inherence', or the taking on of another's burdens. For Williams, a committed if unusual Christian, this was theologically justified as it was a disciple's duty to follow the path of Christ, the ultimate substitute.

How does this work in practice? If you are worried, or grieving, or in pain, ask a brother or sister to carry it for you. Williams believed this brought a genuine lessening of the suffering. In turn, you carry the burden for someone else, feeling it but in a lesser way than the original sufferer.

Not every Inkling agreed that this was possible or desirable. I wonder if this is what Tolkien had in mind when, at one of the darkest points of *The Lord of the Rings*, trapped in Mordor, Sam begs Frodo to let him carry the Ring for him. Frodo's anguished reply is that he 'must carry the burden to the end'. Sam can't come between him 'and this doom'.[26]

While the magical aspect of the co-inherence might not appeal, Williams could be on to something in believing that sharing a burden with a trusted friend or therapist does lessen the load. It's worth considering for any trouble you might be facing.

My favourite aspect of Williams, however, lies in his extraordinary storytelling. His novels cover the gamut of genres from Indiana-Jones-style treasure hunting, to ghost stories, to philosophical thrillers. One theme that reoccurs is the battle over an object of spiritual power. In *War in Heaven* it is the Holy Grail; in *The Greater Trumps* it is an ancient pack of Tarot cards and figurines. In *Trumps* the Tarot is used to reveal the protagonists' spiritual qualities and exposes their moral character. The pack of cards is connected magically to a special table of figures, a three-dimensional image of the drawings. Most people see the still point in the centre as the figure of the Fool. He stays still while all the other figures dance around him. Sybil, an older woman and the wisest of the characters in the novel, however, sees that a golden light comes from among the images 'from the figure of the Fool who moved so much the most swiftly, who seemed to be everywhere at once'.[27] This represents Christ who is the still point at the centre of everything, while also 'everywhere at once'.

In 'Burnt Norton', one of *Four Quartets*, T. S. Eliot uses an image that might have been inspired by Williams:

> At the still point of the turning world. Neither flesh
>   nor fleshless;
> Neither from nor towards; at the still point, there the
>   dance is.[28]

WEEK 2: WEDNESDAY

Eliot's poems take a lot of pondering but I find thinking of Williams' image of the dancing figures illuminates this phrase for me. Jesus is at the centre, in the dance with us, but also in every move of the dance.

The image is a powerful answer to a phrase often used to characterize modern times. It comes from Yeats' 1920s poem 'The Second Coming':

> Things fall apart; the centre cannot hold;
> Mere anarchy is loosed upon the world.

It's a bleak vision of disintegration. Williams (and Eliot) counter Yeats by urging us to see that the Fool/Christ is at the centre holding it all together.

Reflection

What is at the centre of your life? Let today be the day when you recommit to de-centring the things that burden you and putting Christ back at the heart.

Read Matthew 11.28–30.

> Come to me, all you that are weary and are carrying heavy burdens, and I will give you rest.

Thank you, Jesus.

JG

THURSDAY

Golden Past

C. S. Lewis, *Prince Caspian*

Time passes very differently in Narnia. When Lucy returns from her first trip through the wardrobe she calls out to her brothers and sister: 'It's all right ... I've come back.' Because she has been in Narnia for hours, she assumes that they will have been worrying about her and wondering what has become of her. But in fact no time has passed at all in her own world so that Peter replies: 'You'll have to hide longer than that if you want people to start looking for you.'[29] When the four children finally leave Narnia at the end of the story they are adults, but on passing back through the wardrobe they emerge as children. As we have seen, when they are summoned back to Narnia at the beginning of *Prince Caspian*, they discover that hundreds of years have passed and their palace of Cair Paravel has been reduced to rubble.

At first they fail to recognize the ruined remains as belonging to Cair Paravel. It is Susan's discovery of a small golden chess piece, just like one they used to play with, that enables Peter to make the connection. The chess knight is of ordinary size but extraordinarily heavy, since it is made of pure gold. Its eyes are two tiny rubies, although one of them is now missing. Lucy notices its similarity to the golden chessmen that the children played with at Cair Paravel, when they were Kings and Queens of Narnia. This is the final piece in the puzzle which leads Peter to realize that the layout of the ruins, the orchard and the chess piece all indicate that this is all that remains of the great castle where they reigned happily and peacefully.

WEEK 2: THURSDAY

Susan's discovery of the chess piece triggers a wave of nostalgia as she recalls the wonderful times she enjoyed, playing chess with fauns and good giants, being serenaded by the mer-people singing in the sea and riding her beautiful horse. The gold of the chess piece symbolizes the golden age of Cair Paravel, a time of joy and peace, starkly contrasted with the present, in which Cair Paravel lies in waste and the chess pieces scattered, damaged or lost. The golden chess piece recalls the golden chequers that the Norse gods played with that are found lying on the grass in the vision of the new world described in the Seeress' Prophecy in the poem known as *Völuspá*. While the golden chequers recall the past and a time that is now irretrievably lost, they are also a symbol of hope, pointing forward to a future in which the fields will grow again, all ills will be healed and the beloved god Balder will return.

While the discovery of the chess piece saddens Susan by bringing back happy memories that are now past, it is the key to preparing the children for a new challenge. Having discovered the steps down to their ancient treasure chamber, they find their suits of armour, brooches, coronets and chains of gold that they wore when they were Narnian royalty. The precious treasures are so covered with dust that, without knowing what they were, the children would never have recognized their value. The realization makes the children sad, since everything seemed 'so forsaken and long ago'. Realizing that they don't have long before Edmund's torch battery runs out, they walk straight past the rich and splendid jewels and head for the end of the chamber, where they stored the gifts given to them by Father Christmas in *The Lion, the Witch and the Wardrobe*, recognizing that they will likely need them in whatever adventure lies ahead. There is a time for reminiscing about the past and recalling its joys and sorrows, but there is also a time for looking to the future. The small golden chess knight is a reminder of a time of peace and leisure, where the children could engage in play and sport. But a time is coming when they will need to become real knights once more, taking up the gifts that Father Christmas gave them, with the solemn warning that they were 'tools, not toys'.

Reflection

Are there memories of the past that simply drag you backwards? Or are there moments and past gifts that when you recall them give you courage now?

Read Ecclesiastes 3.1:

> For everything there is a season, and a time for every matter under heaven.

SH

FRIDAY

The Screwtape Letters – Living in the Present

C. S. Lewis, *The Screwtape Letters*

In our reflections on the moment of decision in *The Great Divorce* we touched on the importance of the present moment, of making the choice *now*, while it can be made, doing the right thing *now*, while it can be done. The angel says: 'This moment contains all moments.' Lewis brings these ideas about Time and eternity, and about the almost sacred character of the present moment 'the now' as we experience it, in letter XV of *The Screwtape Letters*, a letter which is essentially an extended meditation on Time.

The key statement, on which the whole meditation turns, comes near the beginning of the letter:

> The humans live in time, but our Enemy destines them to eternity. He therefore, I believe, wants them to attend chiefly to two things, to eternity itself, and to that point of time which they call the Present. For the Present is the point at which time touches eternity.

Here we have an insight that is at once practical and mystical. Practical, because if any good is to be actually done it must be done in the present moment. It's no use looking at the past, which, as Lewis says elsewhere in this letter, 'is frozen and no longer flows'. We cannot change or affect the past. Neither is it any practical use to keep postponing the good deed, the kind word, the act of mercy to some indefinite future when we might be feeling better or hope to have a more opportune moment. The future is unknown and indeed not yet real, and to make that the location of all our kindness, well-doing, or even happiness, is to pour all that moral energy into a void, to dissipate it and do nothing. As Screwtape, offering the tempter's perspective, says later in this letter:

> We want a whole race perpetually in pursuit of the rainbow's end, never honest, nor kind, nor happy now, but always using as mere fuel wherewith to heap the altar of the future every real gift which is offered them in the Present.

Notice the language of 'gift' here: 'every real gift which is offered them in the present'. Each moment arrives as a gift from the hand of God. Each moment, as it becomes present to us, is the only moment in which we can love God and neighbour, but it is also the only moment in which we can be happy, in which we can enjoy what we receive. We must receive it, enjoy it, strive to do well in it, and then gladly let it go without regret, without hankering back for it in the past. If we do that we miss the gift being given in the next moment, a moment we will have wasted in the backwards glance. And if we miss so much present goodness in nostalgia for the past then how unnecessarily we torment ourselves in anxiety, over things that may not come to pass. We can anticipate a crisis, but we cannot imagine the strength we may be given in the moment the crisis comes if only we will receive it in the moment it is given.

Jesus has of course already made all this clear to us in the Sermon on the Mount. '[D]o not worry about your life, what you will eat or what you will drink ... ' and more specifically 'do not worry about tomorrow, for tomorrow will bring worries of its own' (Matthew 6.25 and 34). Paul takes up the same theme in Philippians 4.6: 'Do not worry about anything, but in everything by prayer and supplication with thanksgiving let your requests be made known to God.'

But Lewis' insights in this letter are mystical as well as practical. 'The present is the point at which time touches eternity';

WEEK 2: FRIDAY

and, as he says elsewhere, 'the present is all lit up with golden rays'. This insight is sometimes called 'the sacrament of the present moment'. To be still and abide, breath by breath, in God's beautiful present of the present moment, is to find ourselves, in the deepest sense, continually in his Presence.

Reflection

Re-read Philippians 4.6 and offer to God, place into his hands for him to carry, whatever feared or imagined future is causing you anxiety.

Still and centre yourself, become aware of the rhythm of your breathing and try to rest in the present moment of each breath knowing that God is abiding there with you.

MG

SATURDAY

Frodo and Gandalf – All We Have to Decide Is …?

J. R. R. Tolkien, *The Fellowship of the Ring* and 'The Battle of Maldon'

You would not be alone in thinking that we are living at a moment when things seem to be in the balance, perhaps tipping in the wrong direction. Many of us find ourselves echoing Frodo's plea: 'I wish it need not have happened in my time.' Frodo has just found out the very bad news that he is in possession of the ultimate weapon and prize of the enemy – the Ring. Gandalf's answer is very wise and resonates with so many of us. He advises acceptance as we can't change what is given our generation, saying, 'so do all who live to see such times. But that is not for them to decide.' He goes on, 'All we have to decide is what to do with the time that is given us.' Not many remember past that to the next sentence, but he says, 'already … our time is beginning to look black'.[30] He doesn't tell Frodo, 'Don't worry, you'll get your happy ending'; he is trying to help his friend face impossible odds with resilience and courage.

Almost every generation, some very particularly, have felt they were living in dark times. The rapid pace of change, pandemics such as Covid-19, the impact of the changing climate, war and the rumours of war: these are familiar and stressful prospects. One of the greatest fears of a parent is our country going to war and adult children being sent off to fight – something many mothers and fathers around the world are facing now. It once might have seemed far off; now it doesn't feel unimaginable. It would be great to have a delete button to get rid of such threats, but that doesn't lie in our power.

What can we do? This is where Tolkien can help. He faced at least two occasions when the skies turned black – World War One and World War Two – for himself and then for his sons. He wrote this sentence in the late 1930s as he saw countries gearing up for war against the forces of Nazism. Having passed through the Somme, the bloodiest battle for British troops in World War One, he knew such times could not be wished away, no matter how hard you tried. What he offers in response is a Stoic philosophy with a Christian twist. It is how you fight the battle, not whether you win. As Galadriel later tells Frodo, she and Celeborn have been fighting 'the long defeat', not expecting victory but prepared to diminish and go into the West. Here Tolkien is nodding to the idea of Ragnarök, the end times, from his favourite Norse myths. In this final battle, the point is not being on the winning side, but on the right side. You fight alongside gods and men, not on the giants' team.

Or as one of Tolkien's favourite Anglo-Saxon poems puts it, in Tolkien's own translation that he was working on at this time: 'Each mind shall be the sterner, heart the bolder, each our spirit greater as our strength lessens!'[31]

But before we leave ourselves in grim Stoic acceptance, let us remember the Christian twist of eucatastrophe – the sudden joyous reversal. It is there in Gandalf's words: the time that is 'given' to Frodo. He hints that there is another hand behind events, giving us the moment. With this hope, you can hope for the best. Gandalf later muses that, though the encounter of Frodo with Gollum seems bad news: 'Let us remember that a traitor may betray himself and do good that he does not intend. It can be so, sometimes.'[32] It proves to be true. And Elrond offers an empowering notion: 'Yet such is oft the course of deeds that move the wheels of the world: small hands do them because they must, while the eyes of the great are elsewhere.'[33]

Reflection

As we gear up for spiritual battle in our present day, what kind of warrior should we be?

Be merciful, have pity, be courageous – these are the lessons of *The Lord of the Rings*. When in doubt, stick to those values and you win even if you lose.

In the light of that, what do you have to decide to do with the time you have been given? What can your 'small hands' do to change things for the better?

Read Hebrews 12.1–2.

JG, MG, SH

WEEK 3

Sub-creation – Creativity and Creation Stories

A beech tree in Wytham Woods, Oxford

SUNDAY

Phantastes and Holiness

George MacDonald, *Phantastes*;
Shakespeare, *A Midsummer Night's Dream*;
C. S. Lewis, *Surprised by Joy*

We have already noticed how works of imagination, stories and poetry have a way of reaching more deeply into us than rational argument, even, and especially, in matters of faith. There is something about holiness itself, about the numinous and awe-inspiring presence of God that shies away from the interrogations of the logical mind but reveals itself to us more fully when our imagination is aroused and at work. Shakespeare put it very well when he wrote, in *A Midsummer Night's Dream* that,

> imagination bodies forth
> The forms of things unknown, the poet's pen
> Turns them to shapes and gives to airy nothing
> A local habitation and a name.[34]

Sometimes a story or a poem 'bodies forth', gives form and meaning to, glimmerings or intuitions that might otherwise escape us. If we have had that experience of being ushered into the presence of something holy while reading the works of the Inklings, then it is good to know that they too shared this experience, that it was part of their inspiration when they came to write for us.

C. S. Lewis famously tells the story, in *Surprised by Joy*, his spiritual autobiography, of how George MacDonald, the great Victorian fantasy writer, did that for him. Lewis tells of how, apparently by chance, just browsing in a second-hand bookstall in

Leatherhead station he picked up a copy of George MacDonald's *Phantastes: a Faerie Romance*. It was a turning point in his life, one of those moments of joy, which led him a long time afterwards to his faith in Christ. Not because the book he read was in any obvious way about Christ, but because, in some sense which he could hardly put into words, it 'baptized' his imagination. Everything associated with this turning point in his life is still vivid for Lewis decades later, even the names of the railway stations, listed like a litany by the station porter: 'I can still remember the voice of the porter calling out the village names, Saxon and sweet as a nut – "Bookham, Effingham, Horsley train".' Then he tells us how the outward and visible journey on the train with his book, and his further reading of it when he got home, was also an inward and spiritual journey into a new country, a country that bordered on heaven: 'It is as if I were carried sleeping across the frontier, or as if I had died in the old country and could never remember how I came alive in the new.' He goes on to say that 'all was changed. I did not yet know (and I was long in learning) the name of the new quality, the bright shadow, that rested on the travels of Anodos. I do now. It was Holiness.'

How MacDonald would have rejoiced (and I am sure did rejoice in heaven) to know that his book was having this effect! MacDonald had offered his imagination and his powers as a writer to God and then learned to trust the stories as they came. Not to impose an allegory, or to explain a single meaning, but to let the stories, and the images that came with them, do their own mysterious work. For Lewis, the effect can best be described as re-enchantment, not just in the magical world of the story but in the real world in which he lived: a veil was being lifted, the dark spell of mere materialism was being broken. Lewis tells us:

> When the great moments came I did not break away from the woods and cottages that I read of to seek some bodiless light shining beyond them, but gradually, with a swelling continuity (like the sun at mid-morning burning through a fog) I found the light shining on those woods and cottages, and then on my own past life, and on the quiet room where I sat ... I saw the

bright shadow coming out of the book into the real world and resting there, transforming all common things and yet itself unchanged.

He sums the whole experience up in a single sentence: 'That night my imagination was, in a certain sense, baptised; the rest of me, not unnaturally, took longer.'[35]

Reflection

Read Isaiah 25.6–9.

Have you had an experience when the veil is lifted and you seem to see things in heaven's light? Was it in church, or out in nature or both? Isaiah speaks of a 'holy mountain'; where have you found the holy mountains in your life?

MG

MONDAY

Mythopoeia and Sub-creation

J. R. R. Tolkien, 'Mythopoeia' and 'On Fairy-Stories'

Mythopoeia, from a Greek word meaning 'myth-making', refers to a kind of literary fiction in which archetypes and themes drawn from traditional myths are employed in other kinds of fictional writing, such as fantasy or science fiction. The word was not coined by either Lewis or Tolkien, although its use is particularly associated with their writings. For Tolkien the word is closely linked with the concept of 'sub-creation', which, although it predates Tolkien, has a separate sense in the *Oxford English Dictionary* referring particularly to his usage: 'spec. J. R. R. Tolkien's word for the action or process of creating a fully realized and internally consistent imaginary (or "secondary") world.'

Tolkien sets out his understanding of these two key terms in a poem called 'Mythopoeia' and in his essay entitled 'On Fairy-Stories'.[36] In the poem Tolkien offers a defence of sub-creation and the 'little maker's art', refusing to cast down his own 'small golden sceptre' and embrace a dreary world in which there is no place for imagination and creativity. The poem is addressed to 'one who said that myths were lies and therefore worthless, though "breathed through silver"'. This is a reference to C. S. Lewis, the Misomythus, 'or Myth-hater', following a conversation between the two men and Hugo Dyson that took place on Addison's Walk at Magdalen College in September 1931 (the conversation is discussed in more detail later in this book). But, in addition to its role in convincing Lewis of the importance of myths as vehicles of truth, this poem is significant as a statement of Tolkien's understanding of the role of the sub-creator and in offering an apology for the vocation of the myth-maker.

In the poem, Tolkien argues that a purely rational and scientific view of the world severely limits man's appreciation of creation. To look up at the night sky and see only balls of flaming gas is to see only a very reduced vision of the created world, missing out on the imaginative value conveyed by mythical views by which the firmament becomes 'a jewelled tent, myth-woven and elf-patterned'. According to this poem, the creative act is a God-given gift and one that we should continue to exercise, despite our fallen status. Man may be dethroned, having been cast out from Eden as a result of the fall, but he is not dis-graced – neither cast out into a state of dishonour nor cut off from God's grace. We still wear our robes of lordship, even though they are now ragged. Despite this separation from God the Creator, we have held on to our right to emulate him through sub-creation: 'The right has not decayed / We make still by the law in which we're made'. It is that sub-creative power that means that it is through man that the single white light of truth may be 'splintered ... to many hues'.

In the essay, Tolkien offers a defence of the application of the sub-creative art to the genre of fantasy. Where critics have dismissed such writing as illegitimate, suspect or juvenile, Tolkien argues that fantasy is a natural human tendency, offering the reader a chance to see the familiar world in a new way, escape from modernity and satisfy our oldest and most deep-seated desires. Far from opposing or denying reason, fantasy sharpens rather than obscures our appreciation of scientific truth. Of course, fantasy can be done badly or can be used to create false gods, but the potential to become a sub-creator is an important human right – we can become creators because we are made in the image and likeness of a divine Creator.

WEEK 3: MONDAY

Reflection

Read Colossians 1.16:

> [F]or in him all things in heaven and on earth were created, things visible and invisible, whether thrones or dominions or rulers or powers – all things have been created through him and for him.

Make a creative prayer today – be it a poem, a line or two, a picture, or a photo. Enjoy your power of sub-creation!

SH

TUESDAY

It All Began with a Picture

C. S. Lewis, 'It All Began with a Picture'

Authors are liars – that is what C. S. Lewis writes when asked how they create their stories. In his little essay 'It All Began with a Picture ...' Lewis warns that 'you must not believe all that authors tell you' when you ask them where an idea came from, or how they sat down to write their books. Before you cancel your tickets for the next literary festival as being populated with fibbers, he adds that this is not because they mean to lie but because they are 'too excited about the story itself to sit back and notice how [they are] doing it'. He makes the comparison to tying a tie. Done on instinct for years, if you stop and think about it, 'you find you can't tie it'.[37]

I imagine there are many skills in life for which this is true. If you are a painter, you can't paint-by-numbers to explain what you do. If a gardener, once you've got growing seasons of experience as to what plants go well in what areas of your garden, what colours look good together, it would be hard to distil it for an amateur who wants to cut all the corners and have an instant display of flowers and vegetables. Or maybe you are the talented cook who barely looks at a recipe but knows from the contents of the fridge and cupboard what will go well with what and how to prepare the dish.

All of us are likely to have some area of our lives where we are a budding creative genius – go on, admit it to yourself!

Having warned us about the lying, Lewis goes on to say: 'One thing I am sure of. All my seven Narnian books, and my three science fiction books, began with seeing pictures in my head ...'

I'm not sure how much we are meant to believe him after the 'all-authors-are-liars' comment but let's go with him on this. According to Lewis, 'The *Lion* all began with a picture of a Faun carrying an umbrella and parcels in a snowy wood', an image that popped into his head when he was a teenager. Decades later, when he was 'about forty', he decided to try to make a story about it.[38]

There are several thoughts to be drawn from this. First, he waited until he was 40 to be ready to write the story that became Narnia. That's encouraging to those of us who have an inkling of something we've long wished to try: a new hobby, a more fulfilling job, or a lifestyle change. We can look at the delay as maturing rather than missing the boat. We can start now on our new creative venture.

The second thought, which is connected, is that it is true, and not true that it 'all began' with one picture. Rather than Lewis' tie, let's think of creating something as driving a car. If you start thinking about it, you stop being able to do it – that's why learning to drive is so hard at first. But when you drive the car, the lessons are still there behind you. There's more to it than starting the engine – or thinking about a picture that has been in your mind since you were a teenager; you need the practice and the wisdom to be a good and safe driver. That might well be the same as the necessary maturing period. You are now the person you need to be to set off on the adventure.

In midlife, I now appreciate the fact that, unlike the child heroes in the Narnia stories, Tolkien had a penchant for main characters who are in their 50s, a fact masked by the casting of a young actor in Peter Jackson's *The Lord of the Rings* films. If you go back to the books, you'll see that Bilbo and Frodo both set off in that decade. The human equivalent to that hobbit age would be your 30s. Even Jesus waited until he reached that age before beginning his ministry. Perhaps he too needed a period of maturing and seasoning before he was ready to begin?

Reflection

What adventure have you been putting off?

Read Luke 3.23, 4.14–21.

JG

WEDNESDAY

Tolkien and the Music of Creation

J. R. R. Tolkien, *The Silmarillion*

I remember the rush of excitement when I first heard of *The Silmarillion*, and then the thrill when it was published, in 1977, four years after Tolkien's death. At last, we had the creation story of Middle-earth itself. The opening chapter, 'The Music of the Ainur', was both moving and mysterious. It had never occurred to me to think of creation itself as a kind of music. Eru, God himself, also called Iluvatar, declares to the Ainur, the angels, a great musical theme, but he devolves to them, and to their own creativity, the making of that music – already Tolkien's vital theme of sub-creation is in play. So Eru says to them:

> Since I have kindled you with the Flame Imperishable, ye shall show forth your powers in adorning this theme, each with his own thoughts and devices if he will. But I will sit and hearken and be glad that through you great beauty has been wakened into song.

The Ainur make a great and beautiful music, but even that music is not yet the created cosmos, but only its root, its origin, for Eru takes the music and gives it a new physical expression. He creates the world and then says to the Ainur, 'Behold your music!' We see here the way in which God is the primal creator, the source of all there is, including our own creativity, but that he makes a space for us to be creative too, lovingly to expound and develop the themes he has given us to work with.

But Tolkien does more than explore the theme of Creation, he also addresses Fall and Redemption: the problem of evil, and God's creative answer to it. For Melkor, the highest of the Ainur, the Lucifer of this myth, seeks 'to interweave matters of his own imagining, that were not in accordance with the theme of Iluvatar, for he sought therein to increase the power and glory of the part assigned to himself'. So discord and dissonance are introduced, and their root, as of all evil, is pride. And this is where Tolkien communicates something true and beautiful through his myth. For Iluvatar does not directly interfere, or curtail the free will of his creatures; rather he responds creatively to their evil choices: he introduces new themes that work with and through the dissonance and bring out of it an even greater harmony. Melkor's attempts at disharmony are not silenced but 'taken up' by the new themes and 'woven into its most solemn pattern'. Since that music with its redemptive motifs then becomes Arda, the created world, with its history, we can see this theme and counter theme worked out in the story of *The Lord of the Rings* in the way that even the fallen characters are woven into the redemption. Gandalf intuited that Gollum still had a part to play, and even though he sought possession of the Ring, he contributed to its destruction and the achievement of the quest, stepping in just at the point when Frodo could go no further. It is indeed just as Iluvatar says to Melkor:

> And thou Melkor shalt see that no theme may be played that hath not its uttermost source in me, nor can any alter the music in my despite. For he that attempteth this shall prove but mine instrument in the devising of things more wonderful, which he himself hath not imagined.

I loved this creation myth so much that I wished that it were true, so you can imagine my joy when later in my life, as I returned to my Christian faith, I discovered that that notion of a primal heavenly music was there in the Scriptures – 'When the morning stars sang together, and all the sons of God shouted for joy' (Job 38.7, KJV) – and in Christian tradition, in the idea of the heavenly 'music of the spheres' which only our fall prevents us from hearing.

Reflection

Re-read one of the biblical accounts of Creation, either Genesis 1 or Job 38 or both, and take time to reflect on the sheer splendour and majesty of the creation in the midst of which you find yourself.

Now listen to a favourite piece of classical music and try to imagine what kind of a world that music would suggest, if it could be 'bodied forth'.

MG

THURSDAY

Creation of Narnia

C. S. Lewis, *The Magician's Nephew*; Ovid, *Metamorphoses*; John Milton, *Paradise Lost*

In *The Magician's Nephew* Digory and Polly find themselves in the privileged position of witnessing the creation of Narnia. It all begins with the sound of a faraway voice. Although there are no words, hardly even a tune, the singing is the most beautiful sound the children have ever experienced. Then the voice is joined by numerous others. At the sound of these 'cold, tingling, silvery voices' innumerable stars suddenly appear in the sky, transforming it from pitch black to a blaze of light. As the stars appear, so the high-pitched voices fall silent, while the deep voice continues to sound. Next, they witness the sky gradually turning pale and revealing the outlines of the hills on the horizon. As the sun sends out beams of light across the land, the singer himself becomes visible: it is Aslan, appearing majestic and bright as he faces the sun, with his huge mouth open in song. As the music switches to a softer, more lilting tone, grass begins to spread out across the land, heather covers the dark slopes of the hills, and trees and flowers, daisies, buttercups, lilacs and wild roses, gradually emerge from the fertile earth.

Polly is the first to make the direct connection between the song and the creation they are witnessing, so that it appears as if everything they see is coming out of the lion's head. This realization gives her a thrill – she is so excited by what she is observing that there is no time to feel frightened. Uncle Andrew and the Witch, however, are terrified and desperate to get hold of the rings that will enable them to flee the scene. Andrew's concerns are focused on his sense of having been poorly treated and on his social status and reputation. Finding Andrew's complaining interfering with his ability to listen to the music, the Cabby silences him: 'Oh stow it, Guv'nor, do stow it ... Watchin' and listenin's the thing at present; not talking.'[39]

The Witch's terror prompts her to throw the iron bar that she has ripped from the London lamp-post at Aslan, though it has no effect on the lion. When it falls onto the fertile soil, the bar grows into a lamp-post, prompting Uncle Andrew to wonder at the commercial possibilities of a land where one could plant scrap metal and watch it turn into brand new railway engines and battleships. Meanwhile, out of the earth appear animals of all kinds, sizes and shapes: moles, dogs, frogs, panthers, leopards and stags, with antlers appearing first, and even an elephant, whose colossal size causes the earth to shake as he pushes his baggy legs up through the surface.

The scene recalls the account of the creation of earth narrated in Genesis 1, while also drawing on similar scenes in Ovid's *Metamorphoses* and Book VII of Milton's *Paradise Lost*, from which Lewis borrows the idea of the animals pawing their way out of the earth's 'fertile Woomb'. There is, however, a striking difference in that the Narnian creation is witnessed by spectators. While the children and the Cabby are transfixed by the beautiful music and the majestic lion, Uncle Andrew becomes increasingly agitated and uncomfortable. Terrified by the idea of a lion singing, and detesting the way the song made him feel, Andrew convinces himself that the lion is only roaring like an ordinary lion in a zoo. The longer and more beautiful the song, the harder Uncle Andrew works at forcing himself to believe that it is roaring. And, as the narrator notes, the problem with trying to make yourself stupider than you really are is that you very often succeed. The result is that, when Aslan calls on Narnia to awake, love, think, speak, all that Andrew hears is snarling and roaring. And, instead of attending to the beasts' response, he hears only the sound of barking, growling and howling. Instead of feasting his eyes on this wonderful scene, his focus is turned in upon himself – 'But what about *me?*' he complains. 'They don't seem to think of that. No one thinks of *me.*'

Reflection

Can we be guilty of behaving like Uncle Andrew, focusing on ourselves rather than looking at what God is doing around us? By being unwilling to see what God is doing and convincing ourselves that we cannot hear his voice, can we behave like Andrew and close our minds off to what God is saying to us?

Read John 10.27 (NIV):

> My sheep listen to my voice; I know them, and they follow me.

SH

FRIDAY

Daring to 'Incarnate Jesus' – Dorothy L. Sayers

Dorothy L. Sayers, *The Man Born to be King*, *The Mind of the Maker* and *Gaudy Night*

The all-male Inklings lack a feminine perspective. Luckily, you don't have to go far to find one in the shape of Dorothy L. Sayers. She is now most famous for her Lord Peter Wimsey detective thrillers, but she could in another era have been one of the Inklings because she was a friend to several of them, broadcasted popular theology like Lewis and wrote cathedral plays like Charles Williams. As an Inkling adjacent figure, she was the most audacious Christian of them all. Lewis wrote after her death, 'Let us thank the Author who invented her.'[40]

What was it that made her the most audacious? It may seem odd to us now, but she broke the rules in her BBC Radio play cycle *The Man Born to be King*. These were skilful adaptations of the Gospel stories in contemporary language for the wartime audience. The press in the 1940s decided it was new and shocking to depict Jesus in the voice of a modern actor and so whipped up opposition to this 'blasphemous' idea. Fortunately, the BBC didn't cancel the series and it was a hit, making the life of Christ accessible to millions in a new way. The storm proved to be the kind that fitted in a teacup. The drama became a regular Lenten read for C. S. Lewis.

Like the Inklings, Sayers was interested in the theology of creativity. This is given the fullest exploration in her book *The Mind of the Maker* (1941). Sayers suggests the act of artistic creation brings us close to the Genesis moment of 'creation out of nothing'. She gives the example of the poet: he is not obliged 'to destroy the material of a Hamlet in order to create a Falstaff, as a carpenter must destroy a tree form to create a table form'; 'the world of the imagination' is increased 'by a continuous and irreversible process, without any destruction or rearrangement of what went before'.[41] When humans are creative, we are in the heady position of adding to the sum of the world's creativity unfettered by the scientific law that matter cannot be created or destroyed. Go forth and multiply – your ideas!

Her experience of creating characters produces this insight: 'The free will of a genuinely created character has a certain reality,' she writes, 'which the writer will defy at his peril.' Once you have established the character in your mind as a person, you aren't free suddenly to make them act out of character, the selfish man becoming generous, or the kind cruel. It can produce a crisis in a novel if character needs and plot developments part company: 'It does sometimes happen that the plot requires from its characters certain behaviour, which, when it comes to the point, no ingenuity on the author's part can force them into, except at the cost of destroying them.'[42]

The analogy here is to our free will. Imagine yourself as a character in the great story of life. Once your character is established in the mind of the Maker, to make you behave in a different way, even for a good plot twist, would destroy you. You wouldn't be you. Your job is to muddle through in character, trying to make the best decisions you can.

Sayers allows her characters of Harriet Vane and Lord Peter Wimsey to grow to the point where rather than destroying them she lets them break the bounds of the detective novel. She follows their romantic story, and explores the cost to them of sending criminals to the gallows (something most detective fiction ignores), as well as championing through Harriet in *Gaudy Night* the academic and intellectual work done by women. This daring to be different was not universally admired. Tolkien, in one of his more waspish moments, declared that after an initial liking he conceived a 'loathing' for Lord Peter Wimsey and 'his creatrix'.[43] He liked his detectives to stay in their lane and not swerve into affairs of the heart. However, I think it a strength, setting Sayers' novels apart from the formulaic detective thrillers of the Golden Age of Crime.

Reflection

What character do you think you might be in the mind of the Maker? Do you need to change lanes to fulfil God's purpose for you?

Read Proverbs 16.9.

JG

SATURDAY

A Preface to Paradise Lost
– C. S. Lewis on Milton

C. S. Lewis, *A Preface to Paradise Lost*

This week we have been looking at some of the creation stories the Inklings composed as sub-creators of their own worlds, but of course they were in different ways drawing on the great creation story of our own world which we are given in the opening of Genesis. That creation story has itself inspired fresh poetry down the centuries and nowhere more so than in John Milton's *Paradise Lost*, in which a story that only occupies three chapters in the Bible blossoms into a 12-book epic poem!

Since we know that Lewis himself drew on those same chapters in Genesis as well as on Milton's elaboration of them for his own Narniad, it is interesting to see what Lewis himself has to say about Milton's poem and especially his craft as a writer.

Lewis' scholarly book *A Preface to Paradise Lost* is, in my view, still the best and most readable work of Milton scholarship. At the heart of the book is Lewis' account of what Milton is trying to achieve *in* us and *for* us, his readers.

It was customary to compare Milton to a master organ player, with the English language as his instrument, but Lewis turns this around and says that *we* are the instrument Milton plays: his imagery reaches deep into us, kindles our imagination and arouses our deepest responses. Writing about how Milton handles the primal image of Paradise itself, central to the whole poem, Lewis writes:

> Whilst seeming to describe his own imagination, he must actually arouse ours, and arouse it not to make definite pictures, but to find again in our own depth the Paradisal light of which all explicit images are only the momentary reflection. We are his organ: when he appears to be describing Paradise he is in fact drawing out the Paradisal stop in us.[44]

This is a remarkable insight, not just into Milton, but into all writing at a really deep level, writing that might be called 'Mythopoeic', working at the deepest levels of myth and poetry, as opposed to mere factual reporting. Lewis' insight into Milton certainly applies to the ways his own and Tolkien's writing works on us. The key insight is the idea that there is 'in our own depth' a 'Paradisal light' which we can be helped to 'find again'. At a level deeper than consciousness the Great Images, or as some would call them the Archetypes, are waiting to be aroused, to be remembered, in some sense realized and brought to bear on our vision of the world. A little earlier in his book Lewis lists some of these Archetypes: 'Heaven, Hell, Paradise, God, Devil, the Winged Warrior, the Naked Bride, the Outer Void.' Lewis acknowledges that some readers may choose a merely personal or psychological explanation for the Archetypes and so explain them away, but he also asks the secular critics to acknowledge that these Great Images might have a spiritual origin and be an instrument of 'real spiritual perception'. Here's how he puts it:

> Whether these images come to us from real spiritual perception or from prenatal and infantile experience confusedly remembered, is not here in question; how the poet arouses them, perfects them, and then makes them re-act on one another in our minds is the critic's concern.

Now let's apply those insights not to Milton, but to Lewis himself, and to Tolkien. Perhaps we can see how some of the most compelling or beautiful 'outward and visible' images in their stories also correspond to something 'inward and spiritual' in us: Ransom's rediscovery of 'the Heavens' instead of mere 'space';

Sam's glimpse, even from the pits of Mordor, of the eternal beauty of the star; the coming of spring to Narnia, and indeed Narnia's creation; the beautiful walled Garden on a mountain top where Digory will find the healing tree. It is worth resting with, dwelling with these images, perhaps revisiting them in our own imagination, for by doing so we may, in Lewis' words: 'find again in our own depth the Paradisal light of which all explicit images are only the momentary reflection'.

Reflection

Re-read Genesis 2 and let the primal images – the Garden planted by God, the four rivers, the Original Man and Woman – appear in your mind. Dwell in them and let them dwell in you. Can you sense that somewhere within yourself there is still an Eden, and still an innocent original type of your own humanity? What difference does that make?

MG

WEEK 4

Conversion, Conversation and Fellowship

The gate to Addison's Walk, Magdalen College

SUNDAY

A Momentous Conversation

C. S. Lewis, *Surprised by Joy*;
Humphrey Carpenter, *The Inklings*

We might like to think of our readings among the Inklings this Lent as a series of encounters with the thought and imagination of these great writers. Perhaps we experience these encounters almost as conversations.

Today and tomorrow we will be reflecting on a momentous conversation that took place between Lewis, Tolkien and Hugo Dyson, all three of them English Literature academics, on Addison's Walk, in the grounds of Magdalen College in September 1931. Lewis had not yet become a Christian, though he had, by force of philosophical argument, accepted that there must be a God, but with no sense that this transcendent God was necessarily connected to Christianity. Looking back, in *Surprised by Joy*, Lewis saw that his mind was deeply divided, between his love of myth and story, almost as a 'guilty pleasure', and his strict philosophical rationalism:

> The two hemispheres of my mind were in the sharpest contrast. On the one side a many-islanded sea of poetry and myth; on the other a glib and shallow 'rationalism'. Nearly all that I loved I believed to be imaginary; nearly all that I believed to be real I thought grim and meaningless.[45]

As the three men strolled around Addison's Walk the conversation turned to myth, and Lewis, for all his love of myths, doggedly asserted that there was no truth in them, that they were lies, though admittedly 'lies breathed through silver'. Humphrey Carpenter, in his book *The Inklings*, describes what happened next:

> 'No,' said Tolkien. *'They are not lies.'*
> Just then (Lewis afterwards recalled) there was 'a rush of wind which came so suddenly on the still, warm evening and sent so many leaves pattering down that we thought it was raining. We held our breath.'

Tolkien took his cue from this breathless hush and went on to show that a tree, as we perceive it, is so much more than just 'a vegetable organism'. It is alive with meanings that flow towards us and from us, meanings of which the tree is an expression. The tree is apprehended imaginatively as well as comprehended rationally, and myth is one of the ways we do that:

> But the first men to talk of 'trees' and 'stars' saw things very differently. To them the world was alive with mythological beings. They saw the stars as living silver, bursting into flame in answer to the eternal music ... To them the whole of creation was 'myth-woven and elf-patterned'.

Lewis however insisted that this idea of imaginative perception and myth still didn't answer his point that myths were lies. Here, according to Carpenter's reconstruction, is how Tolkien responded: 'But ... man is not ultimately a liar. He may pervert his thoughts to lies, but he comes from God, and it is from God that he draws his ultimate ideals.' This leads to the radical idea that, 'not merely the abstract thoughts of man *but also his imaginative inventions* must originate with God and must in consequence reflect something of eternal truth'. There is such joy in this conversation, that you can imagine Tolkien is crystallizing his thoughts almost for the first time with such a receptive audience. He goes on that in making up a myth 'a person is actually fulfilling God's purpose, and reflecting a splintered fragment of the true light. Pagan myths are therefore never just "lies": there is always something of the truth in them.'[46]

This argument got through to Lewis and he began to see that the great story of Christ's Incarnation, Death and Resurrection was in fact one of his favourite myths, the myth of the dying and rising God, actually coming true in the real world. The Christ event was myth incarnate, myth becoming history, and he could respond to it imaginatively with all its mythic resonance, and yet also rely on it as true and actual, accessible to reason, open to rational defence.

A couple of weeks later Lewis wrote to his friend Arthur Greeves to say he had now become a Christian and that his long night talk with Tolkien and Dyson had a lot to do with it.

Reflection

Read Psalm 1.

How does the tree image in this psalm help us to understand our humanity, to understand what it is to be a good person? Can you think of other places in Scripture where trees help us to imagine God's goodness or his kingdom?

MG

MONDAY

Mythopoeia: Tolkien's Response

J. R. R. Tolkien, 'Mythopoeia'

Yesterday we described a momentous conversation between Lewis and his two friends Tolkien and Dyson, but how do we know what really happened? There was, alas, no handy Boswell trotting along beside these great writers to take down their every word.

Well, we know about this conversation largely from the letters both Tolkien and Lewis wrote about it, to their friends and to each other. Most importantly Tolkien wrote to Lewis, continuing the conversation; and, significantly, this continuation was not prose, but a poem. A poem that went to the heart of Tolkien's vocation as a writer. It was called 'Mythopoeia' and we've met this poem before because it is so central to Tolkien's thought and he went on to quote from it in his seminal essay 'On Fairy-Stories'. Fortunately for us the poem has now been published in full in *Tree and Leaf* edited by Tolkien's son Christopher.[47]

The poem opens with a summary of the reductive 'scientism' from which Tolkien and Barfield had been trying to awaken Lewis:

You look at trees and label them just so,
(for trees are 'trees', and growing is 'to grow')

But then, after 30 lines or so of this summary, comes Tolkien's rebuttal:

Yet trees are not 'trees', until so named and seen.

MYTHOPOEIA: TOLKIEN'S RESPONSE

And the human naming and seeing brings an inner response that knows more about the tree, about its meaning, than mere outer observation: As spiritual beings, ours is the response of:

> those that felt astir within
> by deep monition movements that were kin
> to life and death of trees, of beasts, of stars ...

In naming the trees and knowing them at an imaginative and mythological level we are, in Tolkien's memorable phrase: 'panning the vein of spirit out of sense'.

Tolkien then moves on from the poetic imagination's role in perception to the special power it has of 'sub-creation', the power to make our own worlds, with their own stories and mythologies. That power, Tolkien argues, is part of God's image in us, and therefore these sub-created worlds and stories are capable of bearing truth. In a key passage he writes:

> The heart of man is not compound of lies,
> but draws some wisdom from the only Wise,
> and still recalls him ...

Then he writes, perhaps thinking of his own legendarium, as well as the great myths of northern Europe and Britain:

> Though all the crannies of the world we filled
> with elves and goblins ...
> and sow the seed of dragons, 'twas our right
> (used or misused). The right has not decayed.
> *We make still by the law in which we're made.* (My italics)

That last line goes to the heart of Tolkien's theology of Imagination, or Sub-creation. We are made in the image of a Maker. Our own Making must therefore be truthful just as God's is. Our sub-creation must have the same inner consistency, and the same moral framework as the creation in which we find ourselves. If it has that inner consistency, then it will be resonant and perhaps have more truth to tell to us and to its readers than even we are aware of. Tolkien's poem then shifts to a series of beatitudes, of blessings on the legend makers and the myth weavers, in which he clearly sees their art as an act of resistance to the evils of our own times. In one blessing he sees such writers as defying the shadow, and, even in the darkness, weaving on a loom some glints of the coming dawn:

> weave tissues gilded by the far-off day
> hoped and believed in under Shadow's sway.

An early version of this poem ended with two lines of defiance, in which Tolkien himself, like his hero Beren, resists the tyranny of the iron crown of Morgoth:

> I bow not yet before the Iron Crown,
> nor cast my own small golden sceptre down.

Reflection

Read Ephesians 6.10–20.

Paul draws on the image of a warrior girt with shield and sword to describe our Christian life, and immediately following this image he asks the Philippians to pray that he may be 'given utterance', given the right words 'to make known the mysteries of the gospel'.

Think of the stories or poems that have given you courage to resist evil, that have renewed your faith and hope. Are there perhaps passages in the writings of Lewis and Tolkien that have had that effect for you?

MG

TUESDAY

Fellowship and Pilgrimage – *The Canterbury Tales* Leads the Way

Chaucer, *The Canterbury Tales*;
C. S. Lewis, *The Screwtape Letters*

Chaucer's great poem, *The Canterbury Tales*, begins in a pub where 29 pilgrims have gathered to begin their pilgrimage to the shrine of St Thomas à Becket in Canterbury. In the General Prologue that introduces the work, Chaucer describes the group, which is made up of representatives of many of the so-called 'estates': a knight, miller, reeve, monk, prioress, franklin, squire, Wife of Bath and so on. In order to while away the journey, the landlord of the Tabard Inn, Harry Bailly, proposes that they have a tale-telling competition. Each member of the fellowship agrees to tell two tales on the way to Canterbury and two more on the return journey. The teller of the best tale will be treated to a slap-up meal courtesy of the others. Chaucer died leaving this ambitious work incomplete. Instead of the nearly 120 projected tales, just 24 survive (two of which are themselves unfinished).

There are a number of interesting parallels between *The Canterbury Tales* and the Inklings. Like Chaucer's pilgrims, the Inklings would often meet in the pubs of Oxford and frequently exchanged stories followed by frank criticism and evaluation. Where Chaucer's pilgrims reflected the various social groups that made up late medieval England, the Inklings were somewhat more restricted. The majority were members of the Faculty of English, although, with the admission of Robert Havard, Lewis' doctor, Adam Fox, the Dean of Divinity at Magdalen College,

Lewis' brother Warren Lewis after he left the army, along with the occasional visits from Owen Barfield, who left Oxford to join his family law firm, the Inklings came to reflect a greater range of professions. Lewis himself implicitly compared this more diverse membership with Chaucer's gathering of pilgrims when he noted that the Inklings comprised all the estates, except, he added, 'anyone who could actually produce a single necessity of life, a loaf, a boot, or a hut'. Nor did it include any women, unlike Chaucer's medieval fellowship.

Chaucer labelled his group of pilgrims a 'felaweshipe', a word that could also be applied to the Inklings, in the sense of a group or company with shared interests. The term has a further level of significance since it is the word used to describe the members of an Oxford college's governing body; many of the Inklings themselves were fellows of their various colleges. The term is particularly useful in characterizing the Inklings as a group since it clearly distinguishes them from the kind of association that Lewis himself labelled an 'Inner Ring': a group of inwardly-facing, like-minded individuals who associate solely with each other and deliberately exclude others, dismissing them as outsiders. A similar contrast is made between the NICE (National Institute for Co-ordinated Experiments) and the 'Fellowship' gathered together at St Anne's under Ransom's direction in *That Hideous Strength*.

For Lewis, the real risk with such groups is the desire that they can provoke an outsider to join, and the lengths they will go to in order to be accepted. Screwtape well understood the risks and the opportunities that the desire to belong offered to devils seeking to recruit souls for their father below:

> The idea of belonging to an inner ring, of being in a secret, is very sweet to him. Play on that nerve ... Some theories which he may meet in modern Christian circles may here prove helpful; theories, I mean, that place the hope of society in some inner ring of 'clerks', some trained minority of theocrats. It is no affair of yours whether those theories are true or false; the

great thing is to make Christianity a mystery religion in which he feels himself one of the initiates.[48]

For Lewis, the key to avoiding falling in this trap is to make your passion the focus of your working life. This will lead you inevitably into the only circle in your profession that truly matters: the sound craftsmen. And, if you spend your spare time consorting with people you like rather than those you think you should like, or those you want to like you, then you will be at the centre of a group that may look to an outsider like an Inner Ring, but is in fact simply a fellowship group.

Reflection

Who is travelling in fellowship with you?

Read Philippians 2.1–2:

> If then there is any encouragement in Christ, any consolation from love, any sharing in the Spirit, any compassion and sympathy, make my joy complete: be of the same mind, having the same love, being in full accord and of one mind.

SH

WEDNESDAY

Late or Not-Quite Conversions – Thorin and Gollum

J. R. R. Tolkien, *The Hobbit* and *The Two Towers*

When we talk about conversions, most of the world now thinks of building work, such as turning the attic into an extra bedroom. This seems to have little to do with its religious meaning of the most important decision you take in your life. Or does it? Are we not repurposed when we decide to follow Christ? We're no longer the falling-down shed but the stable in which Christ may be born.

Other words for conversion are taking a decision to change. It can be incredibly difficult. Jesus is asked by the rich young man what he must do to have eternal life. Used to buying things, he comes with this mindset. He has ticked off his list of laws to obey but worries there is something missing; however, he is sure he can make up the gap under his own power if he gets a nice tidy answer. Jesus replies, but it is not tidy; it is a revolution of everything the man is used to: 'If you wish to be perfect, go, sell your possessions, and give the money to the poor, and you will have treasure in heaven; then come, follow me' (Matthew 19.21). That's a tall order. The man goes away grieving. In Mark he is 'shocked' and in Luke 'sad'. Jesus has uncovered in the man the belief he can perfect himself. Until he makes himself vulnerable – open to conversion into another kind of person – he won't be able to follow Jesus.

The story appears in the three synoptic Gospels always after Jesus has welcomed the little children to come to him. We've just heard that the kingdom of heaven belongs to such as these (Matthew 19.14). Being ready for conversion is much simpler than we (and the rich young man) make it out to be. You don't need to pass complicated exams; you just need to come to Jesus like a child and realize you need him.

Tolkien gives us two fascinating examples of conversion, one that completes and one that fails, which tell us what might have happened afterwards to the rich young man. Maybe he was like Thorin, the lead Dwarf in *The Hobbit*, and got a late conversion? Thorin becomes consumed by his desire for the golden hoard. He has dragon sickness, thinking his identity rests in the possession of the treasure, particularly the Arkenstone, the brilliant jewel dug from the heart of the mountain. Like the young man, he is ready to walk away from friendship with Bilbo and an alliance with the men of Dale because he thinks the hoard is his. However, he is given the grace of a last-minute conversion. On his deathbed, he reconciles with Bilbo and says the magnificent words, worth far more than the treasure under the mountain, praising his hobbit companion: 'If more of us valued food and cheer and song above hoarded gold, it would be a merrier world.' As he leaves this world to go to 'the halls of waiting', gold no longer has any power over him; he converts to a new appreciation of what Bilbo has been trying to tell him all along: friendship and apologies are better coins.[49]

Or maybe the rich young man chose a darker path? In *The Two Towers*, Gollum doesn't quite seize his chance to convert, but it is *so* close. Tolkien in his letters describes this as the most tragic moment in the story. After Frodo's kindness, Gollum is beginning to change. He is on a new path. Then Sam wakes up, sees him crouching over his master, and accuses him of 'sneaking'. Gollum immediately flips to taking that insult as the excuse to go back to his old identity of 'sneaking about' with malign intent. But for a fleeting moment before that, he touched Frodo's hand in 'a caress', and he appeared as 'an old weary hobbit', 'an old starved pitiable thing'.[50] As Tolkien writes, if only Sam had understood more what was going on between Frodo and Gollum, 'things might have turned out differently in the end'.[51] Like the rich young man, Gollum goes away, grieving and sad for the loss of what he'd once owned: the Ring.

Reflection

Read Matthew 19.13–26.

Do you think there are parts of your faith life where you are more like the rich young man than the children? Offer these to God for conversion.

JG

THURSDAY

The Voyage of the 'Dawn Treader' – Whose Quest Is It Anyway?

C. S. Lewis, *The Voyage of the 'Dawn Treader'*;
J. R. R. Tolkien, *The Return of the King*

Imagine being one of the Inklings. The odds are that you aren't going to distinguish yourself as a household name like broadcaster Lewis or fantasy icon, Tolkien. You might instead be a 'useless quack' – as they nicknamed their much-loved colleague, Dr Havard; or perhaps you will be cut off abruptly before your fame is established as happened to Charles Williams; or you may be chiefly a preserver of the achievements of others, as with Warnie Lewis, C. S. Lewis' brother, and Christopher Tolkien, Tolkien's son and editor.

Owen Barfield in later life was surprised to find he was considered a core member of the group. Theologians started identifying the Inklings as 'the Oxford Christians' with a distinct 'Romantic Theology'. With the Inkling meetings long in his rearview mirror, this gave Barfield pause and he began to ask if there was something in it. He wondered '[w]as there something like ... a development that was also a kind of christening' of the Romantic Impulse 'taking place in that period in Oxford through the minds of these men?'[52] In other words, did the Inklings share a quest without even being conscious of it as a joint enterprise? He wasn't to be the most famous, but he played his part.

In *The Voyage of the 'Dawn Treader'*, King Caspian comes up against the question: whose quest is it anyway? Looking at it from his perspective, he owns the ship, commands the allegiance

WEEK 4: THURSDAY

of all on board, and holds the highest title. Surely, he is to be the hero of the tale?

Yet all along the reader has heard hints that he has mistaken his destiny. Reepicheep, the valiant mouse, tells Lucy and Edmund early on that, though Caspian is seeking the lost lords, the mouse's quest is to go to the 'utter East' where the waves 'grow sweet'. Towards the end of the book, all the lost lords identified, Caspian gets carried away with adventuring, far more exciting than boring old kingship, and wants to go on Reepicheep's quest to the World's End. His declaration is met with opposition from the crew, while Edmund even tries to pull rank on him as a high king from Narnia's Golden Age. Lucy's argument is the best, reminding Caspian of his promise to return to Ramandu's daughter. His response is the age-old one of the dog in the manger: if he can't have it, no one can. Caspian declares the quest is ended and he won't let Reepicheep sail off on his own. Poor Reepicheep says: 'Your Majesty promised ... to be [a] good lord to the Talking Beasts of Narnia.' Caspian's ungracious reply is: 'Talking beasts, yes. I said nothing about beasts that never stop talking.'[53]

Retiring to his cabin in a mood, Caspian has his 'come to Jesus' moment – though in Narnian style it is Aslan appearing in the golden lion's head on the wall to talk to him. Caspian doesn't quite apologize but he is repentant – and most importantly he gets out of the way so that those with a journey still to make can do so. He recognizes that his role is to be the one who makes the success of others possible.

This is the keynote of *The Lord of the Rings*. A support role is the mandate given to the members of the Fellowship apart from Frodo. Aragorn is like Caspian – the king, the one who might be thought to be the most likely hero, who will surely be the main doer of deeds? However, he knows his role is to get Frodo over the finishing line so the Ring can be destroyed, not follow the mistake of his ancestor Isildur and regard the Ring as his quest. More mature than Caspian (he is 87 after all!), Aragorn uses the Palantir (seeing stone) to declare himself to Sauron, not to flaunt his return, but to draw the enemy's eye out of Mordor. Like Jesus, Aragorn comes not to be served but to serve.

Reflection

Read Matthew 18.1–5.

What support roles do you have? Perhaps as a parent to children or caring for elderly relatives, helping a spouse, or as a teacher, pastor, friend. Likely there are times when you find the burden heavy or the task thankless. As we approach Maundy Thursday where we remember Jesus washing his disciples' feet, celebrate and value those roles now as a servant coming to serve.

JG

FRIDAY

The Inklings and Magdalen

Simon Horobin, *C. S. Lewis's Oxford*

Encouragement comes in many forms, sometimes just being together, sometimes going deeper. The Inklings was a group that grew up around the friendship between C. S. Lewis and J. R. R. Tolkien, who first met in 1926 at a meeting of the Oxford English Faculty. The group met twice a week during term time: on Tuesday mornings at the Eagle and Child pub (known to them as the 'Bird and Baby') and on Thursday evenings in Lewis' rooms in the New Buildings at Magdalen College. The pub meetings were generally limited to discussing university politics, telling jokes and exchanging gossip, while the Thursday night meetings were spent reading aloud from works-in-progress, giving and receiving feedback. There was no formal membership, but the core group consisted of Lewis' closest friends and fellow scholars from Magdalen College and the Oxford English Faculty, including eminent academics such as Lord David Cecil, Hugo Dyson and Nevill Coghill. Writing to invite the writer Charles Williams to a meeting, Lewis described the group as an 'informal club' whose qualifications for joining are simply: 'a tendency to write, and Christianity'.

The Inklings flourished during the 1930s and 1940s. Its members were the first to hear extracts from many of Lewis' best-known works. *The Problem of Pain, The Screwtape Letters, Out of the Silent Planet, Perelandra, The Great Divorce* were all subjected to the scrutiny of the Inklings. The group's informality meant that unfortunately no official minutes were taken. As such, we have frustratingly few accounts of a typical Inklings meeting.

From the few descriptions that survive, found in letters written by Lewis or brief entries in his brother's diary, we learn that the mode of debate and tenor of the discussion could be sufficiently heated that an eavesdropper would have assumed that they were 'fell enemies hurling deadly insults before drawing their guns'.[54] While this may seem a surprising way to describe a meeting of fellow-Christians, gathered to share and discuss their writing, it reminds us of the importance of opposition and honesty in friendship. What value would there be in a group who simply endorsed and approved of everything that was presented?

Shortly after their first meeting, Tolkien sent Lewis a copy of a very personal poem he had been writing: 'The Geste of Beren and Lúthien'. Lewis responded very positively, praising the work: 'I can quite honestly say that it is ages since I have had an evening of such delight: and the personal interest of reading a friend's work had very little to do with it.'[55] As if to prove the point that he was not influenced by his friendship with the poem's author, Lewis followed up with 14 pages of detailed comments, explaining how he felt the poem could be improved. Far from seeing friendship as a reason to shun criticism, Lewis felt that it was his duty as a friend to help improve the work. Similarly, Tolkien evidently did not feel obliged to take on board all his friend's criticisms. Reflecting on his various suggestions for revisions to the draft of *The Lord of Rings* that Lewis was the first to read, he recalls how many of these were rejected by Tolkien – '*rejected* is perhaps too mild a word for your reaction on at least one occasion!'[56]

But the group was not just about opposition and antagonism. Another important role the meetings played was encouragement. For many years, Tolkien read to the Inklings passages from what was then known as the 'New Hobbit book'. Following the publication and success of *The Lord of the Rings*, Tolkien acknowledged how much the work owed to C. S. Lewis. While Lewis had relatively little influence over the content of the book, his encouragement was critical to inspiring Tolkien to keep working on the huge project and see it through to publication. For a long time Tolkien had seen the work as a purely private hobby. It was Lewis who convinced him to complete the book and submit it for publication:

> The unpayable debt that I owe to him was not 'influence' as it is ordinarily understood, but sheer encouragement. He was for long my only audience. Only from him did I ever get the idea that my 'stuff' could be more than a private hobby.[57]

Reflection

Who encourages you and whom might you encourage?

Read 1 Thessalonians 5.11 (NIV):

> Therefore encourage one another and build each other up, just as in fact you are doing.

SH

SATURDAY

The Mysterious Great-Great-Grandmother

George MacDonald, *The Princess and the Goblin*

George MacDonald was an important and influential writer for both Tolkien and Lewis. One of the most mysterious and numinous figures in all of fantasy literature is the mysterious 'great-great-grandmother' in his children's classic *The Princess and the Goblin*. G. K. Chesterton said, in his introduction to Greville MacDonald's biography of his father: 'Of all the stories I have read ... it remains the most real, the most realistic, in the exact sense of the phrase the most like life.' We may say that Chesterton is indulging his taste for paradox in calling a fairy tale realistic and lifelike, but he defends that view, in summing the book up as an emblematic picture of the situation in which we all find ourselves. So he writes:

> When I say it is like life, what I mean is this. It describes a little princess living in a castle in the mountains which is perpetually undermined, so to speak, by subterranean demons who sometimes come up through the cellars. She climbs up the castle stairways ... Here a good great-grandmother, who is a sort of fairy godmother, is perpetually spinning and speaking words of understanding and encouragement.

Chesterton goes on, in interpreting the image of the house, to say:

There is – something not only imaginative but intimately true about the idea of the goblins being below the house and capable of besieging it from the cellars. When the evil things besieging us do appear, they do not appear outside but inside.[58]

And that is true, but as in all MacDonald's work, the goodness and holiness of the good and holy characters is far more real and compelling than any depiction of shadow or evil. Indeed, the image 'good great-grandmother' grows and deepens throughout the story as Irene the princess herself grows in discernment to see a little more of who she is. In the first encounter she sees 'A very old lady who sat spinning', though we are told she was beautiful. 'And although her face was so smooth, her eyes looked so wise that you could not have helped seeing she must be old.' We learn that she is a queen and yet she is also at one with the poor: 'There was hardly any more furniture in the room than there might have been in that of the poorest old woman who made her bread by her spinning.'[59]

But as the story unfolds we become aware that this woman is in fact an image of the divine. The greater the need or danger Irene is in, the more deeply she sees and understands the mysterious grandmother. A closer intimacy with the divine is symbolized when Irene, having only seen her 'work room', is invited into the Queen's bedroom and sees the mysterious fire of roses that burns in the hearth:

'I've lighted a fire for you, Irene: you're cold and wet' said her grandmother.
    Then Irene looked again and saw that what she had taken for a huge bouquet of red roses on a low stand against the wall was in fact a fire which burned in the shapes of the loveliest and reddest roses, glowing gorgeously between the heads and wings of two cherubs of shining silver.[60]

The roses that burn and aren't consumed recalls the burning bush, and the image of the fire between the cherubim is clearly an allusion to Isaiah 6. Indeed, just as an angel takes a glowing coal from the fire to touch and cleanse Isaiah's 'unclean' lips, so in this part of MacDonald's story the princess is dirtied and muddy from having run away into the mountains and is also cleansed by the fire. But in a beautiful variation Irene hugs her grandmother, and then:

> Irene saw to her dismay that the lovely dress was covered with the mud of her fall on the mountain road. But the lady stooped to the fire, and taking from it, by the stalk in her fingers, one of the burning roses, passed it once and again and a third time over the front of her dress; and when Irene looked, not a single stain was to be discovered.[61]

Reflection

No single image or emblem is adequate to convey the full mystery of God, but different images or emblems can help in different ways. Isaiah 6.1–8 gives us the glory and majesty, but Psalm 131 suggests we can rest on God as a child on its mother. Re-read those two passages. How have Lewis or MacDonald, in their different ways, suggested both the majesty and the tenderness of God?

MG

WEEK 5

Going Through the Wardrobe – The Importance of Story

Blackwell's Bookshop, the home of stories in Oxford

SUNDAY

Supposal vs Allegory

John Bunyan, *Pilgrim's Progress*; C. S. Lewis, *Letters*

A common criticism of the Narnia stories is that they are merely allegories – generally considered a rather limited artform, in which everything represents something in our own world. But, while that is how a novel like John Bunyan's *Pilgrim's Progress* works, that's not what Lewis intended in the Narnia stories. Instead, Lewis himself explained that he set out to write a 'supposal' rather than an allegory. He began by asking himself the question: 'Let us suppose there were a land like Narnia and that the Son of God, as He became a Man in our world, became a Lion there, and then imagine what would happen.'[62]

For Lewis, the great value of stories is the way they allow their readers to experience ideas rather than simply think about them. In an essay titled 'Myth Became Fact' he notes the impossibility of feeling an emotion such as pleasure and simultaneously studying it. But if you aren't roaring with laughter, how can you genuinely understand humour? If you are suffering from toothache, you will be unable to write. But once the toothache has subsided, how could you write a book about pain? Lewis explains this paradox using the myth of Orpheus and Eurydice. Orpheus was permitted to lead his beloved wife out of the underworld, but the moment he looks back at her, she disappears. We can draw an abstract truth from this story about the impossibility of simultaneously seeing and experiencing, but it is not the only truth that this myth can communicate. If it were, it would be an allegory.

As such, an allegory is like a puzzle that must be solved by the reader to reveal its hidden meaning. Its one-dimensional characters straightforwardly signal the qualities they represent, as in Bunyan's Mr Despondency, held captive in Doubting Castle by a giant called Despair. Unlike allegory, myths are stories from which numerous truths may be abstracted. Instead of presenting the reader with a single message needing to be unlocked, myths instil a sense of longing for something much less tangible – 'like a flower whose smell reminds you of something you can't quite place'.[63] Like many of his critics, Lewis considered allegory to be a limited medium, since authors can only insert ideas that they already know, whereas a myth is of a higher order, since authors can fill it with ideas of which they are not yet conscious.

An encounter with ancient myth was one of the key moments in Lewis' introduction to the concept of 'joy'. As a young man he came across the following lines in Longfellow's poem 'Tegner's Drapa', lamenting the death of the Norse god Balder: 'I heard a voice that cried, / Balder the beautiful / Is dead, is dead' (lines 1–3).

Although he knew nothing of who Balder was at that time, it provoked in him an intense desire for something that he could not describe or name. As he came to know more about the Norse mythology, he was deeply attracted to its stories, as well as those told by the Greeks, Celts and Egyptians. But this created a difficulty for him when it came to accepting the claims of the Christian religion, since he considered it to be just another myth, with its story of a dying and rising god, no different from any of the others. Why should he embrace its claims over theirs?

As we saw earlier, it was a late-night conversation with his friends Hugo Dyson and J. R. R. Tolkien in the grounds of Magdalen College that helped Lewis find an answer to this question. What he came to realize is that, when he encountered a god dying and being revived in pagan myths, he found it profoundly moving, suggestive of meanings beyond his grasp. But, when he met a similar concept in the Christian Gospels, he was unmoved. What he took from his talk with Tolkien and Dyson was an openness to accepting the Christian story as a myth, with all its mystery and suggestive implications, but with one key difference from the Norse, Egyptian and Classical myths: it really happened. But, by becoming fact, he argued, Christianity did not cease to be a myth: 'That is the miracle.'

Reflection

Read 2 Peter 1.16:

> For we did not follow cleverly devised myths when we made known to you the power and coming of our Lord Jesus Christ, but we had been eyewitnesses of his majesty.

How do Peter's words challenge Tolkien and Lewis' understanding of myth?

SH

MONDAY

Freedom of the Creator – The Nature of Middle-earth

J. R. R. Tolkien, *The Nature of Middle-earth*,
Letters and *The Silmarillion*;
Julia Golding, *Cat Among the Pigeons*

There are some big questions that never get a complete answer in this life: the problem of pain for one; the unfairness as the good suffer and the bad flourish; where is God in the vastness of creation? You doubtless have your own list of queries that rise up like nettles in the vegetable patch to sting your faith. There's one major question, though, that might be understood by the practice of writing, and that is: do we have free will?

It's a big'un – a question that underlies the justice system and our responsibility for crimes. Earlier ages might have put this in terms of being one of the damned versus the elect; now we tend to think of scientific explanations for brain formation. Can we help ourselves if we are the sum of synapses and chemical reactions? Is there such a thing as moral responsibility if we had the bad luck to be raised and formed in a certain way that made us into the killer or thief we became?

Society must believe in free will to make justice fair – otherwise we are inflicting penalties on the already damaged. Christianity is founded on having a free choice: you either pick up the cross and follow Jesus, or you don't. If we were trapped by brain chemistry to an inevitable selection either way, it would not be a meaningful decision.

So how are we to understand free will? Our day with Dorothy L. Sayers looked at this question (see Week 3, Friday, p. 82). Working as a novelist, I, like her, often have the experience of developing a plot, imagining characters and then finding they run off on their own adventures. It happened in the second book in my Cat Royal series, *Cat Among the Pigeons*. I'd set everything up and then put my main character in the same room as the villain. She misbehaved, trashed a gentleman's club and had to go on the run. I ran after her, following up with a new research journey as to where she could hide from the repercussions. As Ray Bradbury wrote: 'Remember: Plot is no more than footprints left in the snow after your characters have run by on their way to incredible destinations.'[64]

Tolkien has a good description of this in his working papers, now published as *The Nature of Middle-earth* (2021). 'The author is not in the tale in one sense, yet it all proceeds from him (and what was in him), so that he is present all the time.' You could change 'the author' here to 'God' and you'll see where we are going. Tolkien goes on to describe how the author may have 'general designs' and a 'clear conception of the character' but that is the limit of his 'foreknowledge'. He then describes how many authors have the experience I've described of characters coming alive and doing things that weren't foreseen and that modify the tale to become an integral part of what happens. When the tale is done, the author's foreknowledge is complete and 'nothing can be said, or done, that he does not know of and will or allow to be'.[65] Tolkien's letters show him experiencing this very thing as an author. He writes how, for example, 'Trotter', an early name for Strider, 'all of a sudden ... butted in' and, on another occasion, Faramir walked out of the forest.[66] Tolkien had no idea who or what these characters were while writing the story; it is only at the end that their role seems inevitable and complete.

If God is outside the temporal flow of events, in this analogy he is like an author looking at her book on the shelf and knowing that it all came from her and yet the characters were in a key sense free to develop the story. If you recall Tolkien's music of creation in *The Silmarillion*, there's a musical picture of this as

Iluvatar plays the theme, allows others to modify it, then turns it back to completion. He then lets it play out by running it as the world of Middle-earth into which some of the Valar enter. He is the only one to understand the shape of the whole symphony, knowing even the discordant parts played by Melkor will fold back into the harmony eventually.

It is a beautiful view of free will: we are both held in God's hands while being free to tread our path. We aren't abandoned to make our way as we also have a book to guide us: 'Your word is a lamp to my feet and a light to my path.'

Reflection

Read Psalm 119.97–105.

A lamp doesn't show the whole way but the next steps. Are there decisions you have taken that need God to guide you back onto the right path?

JG

TUESDAY

Bottled Sunshine – Owen Barfield and the Excavation of Words

Owen Barfield, *History in English Words*

It would be wrong to think of the Inklings as only consisting of professors of literature. The club also welcomed historians, doctors, editors, students and, in one case, a solicitor.

Owen Barfield was one of the first Inklings and it was his daughter to whom Lewis dedicated *The Lion, the Witch and the Wardrobe*. He published the first fantasy story among the group, *The Silver Trumpet* (1925) and helped Lewis along his way to becoming a Christian. Barfield's intellectual contribution to the group was as a philosopher with a particular interest in how human consciousness evolved. He remained engaged in this field even as he left Oxford to take up his career in the law.

Like Tolkien, Barfield was a lover of languages. Unlike Tolkien, he didn't construct them; he excavated them. He felt that words were wonderful little packages with the past 'bottled up inside them', like a lump of coal or bottle of wine. Once 'we kindle or drink them' they yield up 'their bottled sunshine'.[67] He thought of language like the best kind of archaeology. Whereas a fossil can only give you the structure of a creature from the past, words can give you access to the mind of the people who spoke them. You can get inside their consciousness.

Have you considered the miracle that is the Bible? We have our 'bottled sunshine' in the Scriptures passed down the generations to give us access to the hearts and minds of the many people who contributed to them: the Psalmist crying out against injustice; the Gospel writer shaping the stories of Jesus' life in words; the letter writer advising the Early Church on how to deal with dissent; the prophets and visionaries seeing six-winged angels or the New Jerusalem. It is a good habit to uncork one of these bottles regularly and have a swig of sunshine.

Barfield, however, reminds us that the words at the time when they were set down might have had a very different meaning from the one we now attach to them – even more so when passed through the filter of translation. Barfield believed you could study the changes in individual words and find a pattern that shows a big shift in the human mindset. He concludes that 'when we reflect on the history of such notions as *humour, influence, melancholy, temper*, and the rest, it seems ... as though some invisible sorcerer has been conjuring them all inside ourselves'. These words used to mean the affect the planets and the external world had on a person but now they have gone down 'into the shadowy realm of thoughts and feelings'.[68]

The writers of the Bible lived in an age when their assumptions about interior and exterior were completely different from our own internalized understanding. When they met with someone suffering from mental illness, for example, they would have looked for very different causes from that which a modern medical practitioner would do. If they were ill themselves, they would have considered what 'humour' (black bile, yellow bile, blood or phlegm) was out of balance in their bodies. They might have undergone bleeding or taken a purgative to restore the balance. This was the common medical practice until the early nineteenth century.

With this different outlook in mind, it is instructive to read the healing miracles of Jesus again. It is strikingly progressive that his treatment is of the whole person, not just the inner or outer cause. In Mark's account of the healing of Bartimaeus, Jesus asks the blind man what he wants, and when Bartimaeus asks to see again, Jesus replies that it is his faith that has cured him. In the account of the miracle in John, Jesus is asked if the cause was the man's or his parents' sin – in other words, is that what is having a malign influence on the man's sight? Jesus replies that it is neither; he was born blind so God's work could be revealed in him. The blind man is restored to the light by the Light of the World.

Reflection

Read John 9.1–7.

Medicine is changing at a rapid rate as we gain new insights to the causes and cures for disease. Our language is also changing as to how we describe illness, particularly mental illness, but also disability. What new insights will you find by reading the Bible with a greater understanding of the changing meaning of words?

JG

WEDNESDAY

What is True? Puddleglum and Plato!

C. S. Lewis, *The Silver Chair* and *The Last Battle*;
Plato, *The Republic*

One of the most memorable episodes in *The Silver Chair* comes when Puddleglum and the two children, having been taken deep into a cavernous underworld ruled by a wicked enchantress, have rescued the prince who was imprisoned by her enchantments and are about to make their escape when the witch suddenly returns and seeks to hold them under a new spell. This new spell is to numb and dull their minds and it is accompanied by hypnotic thrumming on a stringed instrument and a 'sweet and drowsy smell' from a green powder she has flung on the fire. The spell's aim is to convince the children that there is no overworld, no 'up above', no Narnia, and there never was. They strive against the enchantment, then Puddleglum has a break-through by remembering the sun shining in the sky. But the witch replies, 'What is this *sun* that you all speak of? Do you mean anything by the word?' And because there is no sun in the witch's cave, they can only describe it by analogy so they compare it with the lamp hanging in the cave. But, of course, the witch can simply reply that they have seen the lamp and made up a bigger and better version and called it the sun.

In this whole episode Lewis is in fact re-telling a much earlier story, Plato's allegory of the Cave. In Plato's story, told in *The Republic*, Socrates asks us to imagine people who have spent their whole lives in captivity chained in a dark cave. There is a fire behind them, and between them and the fire are people who cast shadows on the wall which the prisoners are facing.

WHAT IS TRUE? PUDDLEGLUM AND PLATO!

They are chained in such a way that they cannot even turn their heads to look behind them, so all they see are the shadows; but they don't know they are shadows, they mistake them for reality. Then Socrates asks us to imagine what it would be like if one of them could manage to turn round and see the fire and the people who cast the shadows, now three-dimensional. He would hardly have language to describe it. And what if he freed himself and got beyond the fire and up a tunnel and out into the upper air and this time saw the sun itself and everything true and real and in its own natural colours? At first he would be blinded by the sun, but his eyes would adjust, and the beauty of the real world, up beyond the cave, would inspire him to return to the cave and try to rescue the people. But would they listen? Would it be too painful to adjust their sight to the brightness of reality, would they prefer the familiar world of shadows and dismiss their rescuer as mad?

The same issues are at stake in Lewis' story and the same analogy of light and shadow. But Lewis takes the argument further. The witch claims that the 'sun' and even Aslan himself are just 'projections', silly stories made up and based only on her lamp and her cat. But brave Puddleglum has an answer. First he sees that the witch is not really using reason, but rather hypnosis and suggestion, and the drowsy powder on the fire. So he tramples on the fire with his bare foot, and then asks the key question: if he and the children are only 'making up' Narnia and the upper world, how is it that they can 'make a play-world which licks your real world hollow'? And then he goes on to a great assertion:

> That's why I'm going to stand by the play-world. I'm on Aslan's side even if there isn't any Aslan to lead it. I'm going to live as like a Narnian as I can even if there isn't any Narnia.[69]

This is a glorious moment in the story especially because we the readers know that there is a Narnia and that the witch has been lying. But when we finish the book, we might look at our own world and ask: Are these the shadowlands? Is there more?

WEEK 5: WEDNESDAY

Reflection

Read 1 Corinthians 8—13.

Plato tells his story to suggest a greater truth, that there is an eternal world far more real than the one we're living in. Lewis also uses Plato's analogy in *The Last Battle*. How does this episode in *The Silver Chair*, or your reading of *The Last Battle*, help you to think about your own faith and your ideas of heaven?

MG

THURSDAY

Witches, Woods and Other Creatures

C. S. Lewis, *Surprised by Joy*;
Julia Golding, 'This house has been ...'

When I was a child, I knew I wanted to write stories. The first I remember was a parallel timeslip story about Epping Forest – the arrival of a Roman road being matched to the cutting through for the M25 which was happening as I grew up just over the hill behind my house. I've always had a special place in my books for wood and trees, somewhat like Tolkien. Becoming a Christian in my teens, I suddenly faced a whole new series of questions about creativity. I was a very earnest young person, a Hermione Granger type. I had this little witch character I'd made up called Erkamona. She had a cat called Vomit. They were anarchic and fun but suddenly I found myself asking if I should write about witches at all, even as a joke. They were evil, weren't they? Or were they?

I was wrestling with what I now see as the problem of the Christian writer versus the writer who is a Christian. One writes apologetics and Sunday School material; the other lives out their faith as best they can and lets it infuse what they do like tea working its way through a pot of hot water.

At university, I was rescued by finding a satisfying theory of creativity in the conversations between C. S. Lewis and Tolkien, and it has stayed with me ever since, freeing up what I do so that if my imagination needs to go into dark and difficult territory (I've written adult psychological thrillers), then that is my quest. And what was that theory? That we are sub-creators, made in the image of the Creator to invent our own worlds, knowing they are but a glimpse of the original creation. That dignifies what we create, be it a novel, a poem, a picture, a patchwork quilt, as they are all part of our nature made in the image of God.

Human creation can cast a powerful spell. As we read earlier, Lewis at 16 picked up a copy of *Phantastes: A Faerie Romance* by George MacDonald at a station bookstall and had his world turned upside down: 'now I saw the bright shadow coming out of the book into the real world and resting there'. In effect, he believed it 'baptized' his imagination, though the rest of him took longer to follow.[70] He went on to do the same for his readers. Many of us meet Aslan before meeting Jesus. Tolkien's evocation of Middle-earth means that his readers find themselves walking in Fangorn, or the Old Forest, or the Misty Mountains, or even Mordor when encountering woods, mountains and industrial landscapes. The 'bright shadow' comes out of the book to make everything more resonant.

The lesson I learned from them was not to worry, to let my imagination create, but let it be baptized too. Faith and values can be the skeleton underlying the writing, it doesn't have to be the face. In short, Erkamona should be free to fly her broomstick without worrying about the internalized thought police.

It is hard to point to where exactly in my novels you can trace this influence – it infuses the whole like the tealeaves. Poetry is a quicker path to illustrate. Bathed in books, they come out into the world surprising me with joy at unexpected times. I wrote a poem on a writing retreat staying in the poet Ted Hughes' house in Yorkshire. We were gifted with a heavy fall of snow and that sent me out walking. This is what I met.

This house has been ...

The house has been on the Snow Queen's sledge,
Lost with Hansel and Gretel in dark woods.
The White Queen Jadis set her wolves upon us
And Saruman brought down Caradhras to block our easy path.

Now the sun rises and all looks innocent,
Trees iced for a too-late Christmas.
Children in red boots hold small fists of snow.
A man in fluorescent yellow strolls with his jacketed dog,
A bright spark of daffodil nosing under sagging brambles.
All talk and marvel, sharing the short-lived miracle
That like a guest is only welcome if it doesn't stay too long.

'This path becomes treacherous,' he says, waving his stick
   in farewell.
The dog flashes his warning and disappears around the bend,
Leaving me to the falling snow,
To wizards and the queens who wish me ill
But melt.

Reflection

Read Exodus 35.30–35.

The passage reminds us that the Lord called members of the Israelites to be craftspeople and their work was highly valued. We are all called to be creative so how do you express your creativity?

JG

FRIDAY

A Spell for the Refreshment of the Spirit

C. S. Lewis, *The Voyage of the 'Dawn Treader'*

The Voyage of the 'Dawn Treader' is my favourite of the Narnian books, and it seems to me that every 'episode' in that episodic book, every story within the story, is rich in wisdom and insight, for this is a book that grows with the reader. One of the loveliest episodes in this book is in Chapter 10 when Lucy, reading the magician's spell book on the mysterious Island of the Voices comes across 'a spell for the refreshment of the spirit'. Refreshment of the spirit is just what Lucy needs at this point in the story, for in the course of turning the book page by page in search of 'a spell to make hidden things visible', which is her errand in the story, she is sorely tempted to say 'an infallible spell to make beautiful beyond the lot of mortals her that uttereth it'. Lucy resists this temptation, though Lewis' description of how the temptation felt seems to be a little nod to the temptation of Galadriel we have already looked at: 'She saw herself throned on high ... and all the kings of the world fought for her beauty.' It is only a picture of Aslan that somehow appears on the illuminated page that helps Lucy to resist. Having resisted one temptation, she gives in to another (as so often happens to us); she says a spell to know what her friends think of her and by magic overhears a friend putting her down. She is upset and angry and a tear falls on to the book. It is then, just when she needs it most, that she comes upon the spell for the refreshment of the spirit.

At this point Lewis does something wonderful. All the previous spells were little formulas to recite – our traditional idea of

A SPELL FOR THE REFRESHMENT OF THE SPIRIT

a spell. But Lewis tells us, of this spell: 'What Lucy found herself reading was more like a story than a spell. It went on for three pages ...' and soon 'she had forgotten that she was reading at all. She was living in the story as if it were real.'

And of course, this is just the spell that a good story casts. The child who is reading this passage, immersed in the story, is there with Lucy as she reads a story in which she herself is immersed. It is *the story itself* that refreshes Lucy's spirit, so deeply indeed that the first thing she wants to do is read the story again, just as we do with the Narnia stories. Indeed this whole Lent Book is exploring the way in which *story itself*, and especially the stories told by great Christian storytellers such as the Inklings, baptize the imagination and speak to the spirit.

But there is more. Lewis gives us certain carefully chosen clues about the story that Lucy is reading. First Lucy says, 'It is the loveliest story I have ever read or will ever read in my whole life.' Then when she tries to remember the story (for she cannot turn back the pages of the magic book to re-read it), she remembers four images: 'It was about a cup and a sword and a tree and a green hill, that much I remember.' Now of course these could all be images in a knightly romance, a story of the grail, but they are also images in the sequence of the Passion: the cup of blessing at the Last Supper, the sword drawn and sheathed in the garden of Gethsemane, where a cup of suffering is not refused; and the tree is the cross on 'a green hill far away', a hymn that Lewis and all his readers would have known. The final hint that the story is the 'God-spell' – the gospel, the story of salvation itself – comes when Lucy, seeing the real Aslan at last and not just a picture, asks him:

> 'Shall I ever be able to read that story again; the one I couldn't remember? Will you tell it to me, Aslan? Oh do, do, do.'
> 'Indeed yes, I will tell it to you for years and years.'

WEEK 5: FRIDAY

Reflection

Can you recall and describe any story which has felt most refreshing and renewing to you after reading it? Are there stories or episodes within the four Gospels that you especially turn to for 'refreshment of the spirit'?

MG

SATURDAY

Through the Wardrobe

C. S. Lewis, *The Lion, the Witch and the Wardrobe*

Oxford is full of doors that lead to all kinds of inviting spaces and exciting opportunities. In St Mary's Passage, just off the busy High Street, there's a doorway that is adorned with two gilded fauns and a carved lion's head. The story has it that, one snowy winter's day, leaving the University Church of St Mary the Virgin via the side entrance, Lewis found himself confronted by the two fauns, the lion's head and, turning right, a Victorian lamp-post. At that moment, it is claimed, the key images for the first of the Narnia stories coalesced in his imagination: the fauns representing Mr Tumnus, the lion's head becoming Aslan and the lamp-post being the original of the one that stands in Lantern Waste – all covered in a blanket of snow following the Witch's spell that makes it always winter but never Christmas.

It's a great story and a gift to Oxford tour guides leading gaggles of tourists around the bustling streets of Oxford during the busy summer months. But it's somewhat undermined by Lewis' own account of the origins of the story, which as we saw began with him seeing a series of 'pictures' in his imagination. These pictures – one of a faun in a snowy wood carrying brown paper parcels and another of a witch on a sledge – first appeared to Lewis when he was a teenager. So, although he waited until his forties to write the story, its central images had occupied his imagination since boyhood.

Doorways like the one in St Mary's Passage are arresting and enticing, almost asking to be opened. Others, however, may be much more mundane and functional, but nevertheless lead us

WEEK 5: SATURDAY

into new experiences and opportunities. Remember how the Pevensie children come to find their way into Narnia: in Chapter 1, the four of them are exploring the vast house into which they have been evacuated during World War Two, when they come across a room that is completely empty, apart from a wardrobe.

> 'Nothing there!' said Peter, and they all trooped out again – all except Lucy. She stayed behind because she thought it would be worth while trying the door of the wardrobe, even though she felt almost sure that it would be locked.

But it isn't locked, and it is through that single act of curiosity that Lucy opens up that very ordinary wardrobe and discovers the world of Narnia.

We can't literally go around opening all the interesting-looking doors we encounter, but we can adopt that same attitude of intellectual curiosity and willingness to explore new places, new ideas and new experiences. When Lucy returns and tells her siblings about her adventures in Narnia, they are so concerned about her sanity that they report the story to the old professor who owns the house. But his response completely flummoxes them: 'How do you know', he asks them, 'that your sister's story is not true?' It's a question that it hasn't even occurred to them to ask, and a further indication of the closed minds that mean that, when they return to the wardrobe to test Lucy's theory, they find nothing but a perfectly ordinary wardrobe: 'There was no wood and no snow, only the back of the wardrobe, with hooks on it. Peter went in and rapped his knuckles on it to make sure that it was solid.'

Why can't the older children find their way into Narnia through the wardrobe? What Lewis seems to be suggesting is that there's a difference between entering the wardrobe in a spirit of open enquiry and going there to confirm your own preconceptions.

The story surrounding the doorway in St Mary's Passage testifies to our desire to associate the magical and mythical world of Narnia with particular Oxford locations, to tie it to Lewis' biography and to the city in a physical way. Lewis, however, saw fairy tales as a way of stimulating a longing in the reader for something beyond the material world, offering a new 'dimension of depth'. Reading about enchanted wardrobes should not make us despise real wardrobes, but instead make all real wardrobes a little enchanted.

Reflection

What doors have been opening for you this Lent?

Read Revelation 3.20 (NIV):

> Here I am! I stand at the door and knock. If anyone hears my voice and opens the door, I will come in and eat with that person, and they with me.

SH

HOLY WEEK

The Ultimate Sacrifice

Wayland's Smithy, an old barrow and empty tomb,
on the Downs near Oxford

PALM SUNDAY

Ransom and the Future of the Planet

C. S. Lewis, *Out of the Silent Planet* and *Perelandra*

Out of the Silent Planet opens with a solitary figure, referred to simply as 'The Pedestrian', seeking accommodation while on a walking holiday in the English countryside. On meeting Devine, an acquaintance from his school days, he is introduced to Dr Weston, a distinguished but ruthless scientist, as Dr Elwin Ransom, the great Cambridge philologist.

In the sequel, Dr Ransom is summoned to Perelandra (Venus) to prevent Weston from corrupting Perelandra's Eve, a beautiful green woman, and bringing about a second Fall. Here the name Ransom becomes especially significant, since Dr Ransom is the means by which the planet will be delivered from Weston. The significance of the name is made apparent to Ransom himself when he hears a deep voice ring out: 'It is not for nothing that you are named Ransom.' As the truth of that comment sinks in, Ransom hears the voice again: 'My name also is Ransom.' In this identification it becomes apparent to Ransom just how much rests on his shoulders. Like the Christian God of his own world, Ransom has been brought to Perelandra to redeem the planet by defeating the Satanic figure of Weston and preventing its becoming cut off from the universe, as happened with the earth, known in the Old Solar language by the name Thulcandra, or 'Silent Planet'.

Ransom, confronted with the enormity of the task that has been placed upon him, prays for a miracle to intervene, only to recognize that he himself is that miracle. He tries to shift the responsibility by convincing himself that, as long as he does his best, the final result is not in his hands. Perhaps the plan was simply that, following his inevitably unsuccessful attempt to prevent the Fall, he would return to earth and publish the truths that he had learned on the planet Venus: 'As for the fate of Venus, that could not really rest upon his shoulders. It was in God's hands. One must be content to leave it there. One must have Faith.' But then he realizes that this is not a moral exercise or a sham fight; the future of this world really does depend on him. This provokes anger in Ransom at the unfairness, even absurdity, of such a position and at the imprudence of a God who had arranged things in such a way that so much could hang on the actions of a man like himself. Did God *want* to lose worlds?

But Ransom goes on to recognize that a world in which humans are free to choose their actions could not be constructed in any other way. Not everyone will find themselves confronted by such momentous decisions, but – just as Eve was free to choose whether to eat the forbidden fruit or resist the devil's temptations – so are humans free to decide whether to sin or not, no matter how serious the ramifications: 'Either something or nothing must depend on individual choices. And if something, who could set bounds to it?'[71] Having given humans free will, God has renounced the power to intervene. If something as small as a stone can affect the course of a river, so can someone as small and insignificant as Ransom determine the future of a whole planet.

Reflection

As Jesus turns towards Jerusalem, so we turn our minds to the paths ahead. While we are unlikely to be called to undertake a task as significant as Ransom, his realization about free will has implications for us all. For how else will others come to know God if not through us?

Read Mark 10.45 (NIV):

> For the Son of Man came not to be served but to serve, and to give his life as a ransom for many.

SH

MONDAY

Digory and the Sorrow of Aslan

C. S. Lewis, *The Magician's Nephew*

The Magician's Nephew is Narnia's creation story, its Genesis. Yet it also contains insights into much else in Scripture. For in his 'supposal' Lewis re-imagines the gospel, so that ideas or images that have perhaps become over-familiar or taken for granted come home to us in a new way.

So it is that in the midst of a story that draws on the imagery of Genesis – the beautiful paradisal garden, the test of obedience, the 'fall' and redemption – we nevertheless get an insight whose roots are in John's Gospel. This comes at a poignant moment when Digory, through whose pride and curiosity Jadis (the future White Witch) has come into Narnia even on the day of its creation and innocence, is given the chance to redeem his folly by going on a quest set him by Aslan. That quest is to travel to a paradisal garden and bring back an apple from the tree at its centre. For from the seed of that apple a tree can be planted in Narnia that will guard and protect it. But ever since Digory entered Narnia and heard his uncle refer to it as 'the land of youth' he has been desperately hoping that perhaps fruit from the land of youth might cure his mother who is dying of cancer (though that word is never used), just as C. S. Lewis' mother Flora was, when Lewis was the same age as Digory in this story. Digory knows that he must accept the quest without setting conditions or trying to bargain with Aslan, and he does so, but then: 'a lump came in his throat and tears in his eyes and he blurted out: "But please, please – won't you – can't you give me something that will cure Mother?"'

DIGORY AND THE SORROW OF ASLAN

Then Lewis tells us that up to this point Digory had only been looking down at the Lion's feet and claws, but 'now, in his despair, he looked up at its face'. And there, to his surprise he sees:

> (wonder of wonders) great shining tears stood in the Lion's eyes. They were such big, bright tears compared with Digory's own that for a moment he felt as if the Lion must really be sorrier about his Mother than he was himself.[72]

This moment of compassion moved me deeply as a child, indeed I remember crying when I read it, especially when Aslan says to Digory: 'My son, my son, I know. Grief is great. Only you and I in this land know that yet. Let us be good to one another.'

Later Digory is tempted by Jadis to steal the apple, and use his magic ring to take it straight to his mother, but he refuses the temptation and stays true to his promise to Aslan. But then in a lovely 'eucatastrophe', as Tolkien would say, Aslan gives Digory a fruit from the tree that was planted in Narnia, and Digory takes it to his mother who is healed. And from the seed of that fruit grows the tree from whose wood the wardrobe is made, for of course Digory is Professor Kirk!

I never forgot this moment in Narnia. Years later, and still not quite a Christian, I finally got around to reading the Gospels, and I came to that moment in John's Gospel when Mary speaks through tears to Jesus about the death of her brother Lazarus and then, in the shortest and most poignant verse in Scripture, John 11.35, John tells us 'Jesus wept.' Suddenly, as I read that verse, I remembered this moment in Narnia, how Digory saw the tears of Aslan and saw that he knew and felt his own sorrow as deeply as he felt it himself, and how, with the Lion's kiss, Digory 'felt that new strength and courage had gone into him'.

In that moment what I had 'known in Narnia', known and cherished, came back as a kind of light that illuminated the gospel itself and many things fell into place. My baptized imagination was teaching and telling me something that my rational mind had not yet attained to but longed to know. I decided to re-read

The Chronicles of Narnia, alongside my first full read-through of the New Testament. A few months later I became a Christian.

Reflection

In many churches, the reading today will remember that Jesus wept over Jerusalem.

Read Luke 19.41–44.

Is there an episode in Narnia that has illuminated a Bible passage for you? Or the other way round? If so try re-reading them side by side.

MG

TUESDAY

Gandalf Comes Back to Finish a Task

J. R. R. Tolkien, *The Fellowship of the Ring* and *The Two Towers*

Have you ever faced a task that you knew you had to finish even though your heart quailed at the prospect? One instance familiar to many mothers is that moment in the hospital delivery suite, labour pains under way for a second child, when you remember, 'Oh yes' – though the actual word may not be so polite – *'this* is what childbirth is like.' The foggy memory clears and you know how the next hours will go. You might look for the exit, but you can't leave as you are committed to going through the process.

Facing a challenge knowing what it will entail takes courage. There's the everyday courage of childbirth, of course, but some have faced extraordinary challenges, that of undergoing taxing medical treatment, or risking your life to rescue someone, or heading into battle, like C. S. Lewis and Tolkien did as young men.

In Holy Week, we read how Jesus returns to Jerusalem to face a task he doesn't want to undergo – but his unwillingness is like childbirth. He knows that his sacrifice will be terrible. In Matthew's account, between Palm Sunday and his arrest, Jesus tells a parable about the vineyard owner's son who is killed by the tenants, and he gives the listeners the image of the rejected stone that becomes the cornerstone. Jesus knows he is still in the middle of that story, waiting for the coming rejection and the killing. Yet he also knows his willingness to stick to the mission will give birth to the most wonderful gift of redemption.

One of literature's most famous returns is Gandalf coming back after his fall into the chasm in Moria fighting the Balrog, a monster of flame and shadow. One of my favourite stories about the 1981 BBC Radio drama adaptation of the novel is that Michael Hordern, playing Gandalf, when he got the script read as far as his death in *The Fellowship of the Ring* and thought that was pretty good pay for a character who only made it into the first third. He was therefore shocked to find he came back and held the whole story together after the briefest of reprieves!

That reminds us that, on first reading, Gandalf's return comes as a shock to the reader and to the characters, a wonderful undoing of what had gone wrong. His reappearance comes as a turning of the tide in the novel. He describes his battle with the Balrog and it does sound like a journey into death, down to a place 'beyond light and knowledge', then up to the highest peak, 'a dizzy eyrie above the mists of the world'. Gandalf throws down his enemy and strays 'out of thought and time'. But Gandalf is no human. He is one of the Maia, an angelic being, and thus doesn't die and pass out of the confines of the world as a man would. Instead, naked, he is sent back – a symbol of rebirth into the world – but he knows it is only for a brief time until his task is done. He experiences it like a rebirth because he takes a while to regain his memories and remember his name. When Aragorn cries out 'Gandalf', he replies 'Yes, that was the name. I was Gandalf.' He then agrees they can carry on calling him by that name, though he has become 'Gandalf the White', not the Grey.[73] This same-but-not-the-same appearance before friends recalls Jesus appearing after the Resurrection to Mary, then to the Disciples in the upper room and on the road to Emmaus – but we are getting ahead of ourselves!

In his return, Gandalf is not meant to be an allegory of Jesus but we can read him as a refraction of the light of the gospel story, a character whose journey may remind us of the True Myth. He does not stride into Mordor wielding superpowers, or fly on an eagle to drop the Ring into the fire without effort; neither did Jesus wave a hand to say our sins are forgiven and disappear into heaven. Gandalf returns to muck in with the Fellowship to see the struggle through to the end, knowing that it might well be in vain as the quest is on a knife edge. Likewise, Jesus returns to Jerusalem to go to the cross – until it is finished.

Reflection

Read Matthew 21.33–44.

It's a tough parable warning us not to reject the cornerstone. Does this put you in mind of a task you have to face? Consider how putting your trust in the cornerstone may help you complete it.

JG

WEDNESDAY

Till We Have Faces – What Do You See?

C. S. Lewis, *Till We Have Faces* and *The Last Battle*

C. S. Lewis wrote an astonishing last novel, *Till We Have Faces* (1956), a re-telling of the Psyche and Cupid myth from the point of view of Psyche's sister, Orual. By then, he had met his wife, Joy Davidman, and discussed the story with her. There is a complexity to the main female characters that is the fruit of this new perspective.

Despite being unfavoured, Orual rises to be a great leader of her own kingdom. However, one incident shatters her life. Her beloved little sister, Psyche, is given as a bride-sacrifice to the god Cupid and goes to live in his secret valley. When Orual visits her, Psyche is radiantly happy, but Orual cannot see what Psyche sees: for robes she sees rags, for wine water, for a husband she fears Psyche is sleeping with a monster. She cries out 'come back! What have we to do with gods and wonders and all these cruel, dark things?'[74] Psyche resists but eventually her sister persuades her to take a light to bed to look on her husband's face. This prohibition is the single thing asked of Psyche, akin to not eating of the Tree of Knowledge in the Garden of Eden. Reluctantly Psyche agrees, but instead of a monster, she finds the beautiful god Cupid and is exiled for disobedience.

What do you see? This is the question in the minds of the Disciples when the woman comes to anoint Jesus' feet in Bethany. In Mark and Matthew's accounts the woman is unnamed. In John, she is called Mary, the sister of Martha and Lazarus. Mary makes the extravagant gesture of anointing Jesus' feet with a pound of pure nard, a costly perfume, and then wipes it away with her hair. Judas, like Orual, can see only the bad: the act is outrageous! Think of the cost! What about the poor? John writes that Judas said this because he wanted the money for himself, but you can imagine others might have been thinking similar thoughts. Feet were usually washed with water, not perfume that cost a king's ransom.

Jesus' response is to look at the intention behind the act. They should leave the woman be. She is anticipating the day of his burial with her gesture, and he warns that they would always have the poor with them, but they will not always have him.

C. S. Lewis is fascinated by the way the same place or action can be perceived by two people as entirely different. 'Foolishness to the Greeks' is a biblical phrase that sums this up. Psyche's belief in a loving god in a beautiful relationship with her is foolishness to Orual. Generosity by Mary is a reckless waste of money to Judas. In *The Last Battle* Lewis gives another picture of this through the stable door. The treacherous Dwarfs still believe themselves in a 'pitch-black, poky, smelly little hole of a stable' whereas the children and King Tirian are in the new Narnia. When offered a feast, the Dwarfs only taste old turnips and cabbages. Aslan gives what I find quite the most terrible sentence in the whole series when he says that the Dwarfs will not let anyone help them. 'They have chosen cunning instead of belief.' The prison they are in is 'only in their own minds', they are 'so afraid of being taken in that they cannot be taken out'.[75]

Many of us will know what it is like to be trapped without any promise of light in the stable. We may have got out, but we will know those who are still in that prison. Poignantly, Susan in the Narniad is the only one of the Pevensies who doesn't get to the new Narnia, dismissing Narnia as a funny game they used to play – though the hint is that it is an adolescent phase in which she confuses growing up with fitting in with her peers. She is putting on blinkers and refusing to remember the truth she once knew.

Till We Have Faces offers hope for stable-dwellers, such as Susan. It is set in an Old Testament world but there is a hint of

New Testament redemption to come. Close to death, Orual has a vision of meeting Psyche, who has passed through her trials to glory. In the dream they meet in Psyche's house with 'no cloud between' them. The god is coming and Orual hears that she (Orual) too is Psyche, she too is beautiful. Orual dies after all her suffering, writing: 'I know now, Lord, why you utter no answer. You are yourself the answer.'[76]

Reflection

Why do you think Susan stopped believing in Narnia?

Read John 12.1–8.

In the darkest times, Mary knew she wouldn't go wrong if she kept her eyes on Jesus, even if she didn't fully understand what was about to happen. She knelt before him rather than standing judging as Judas did. Her actions echo Orual's words: I know now, Lord, why you utter no answer. You are yourself the answer.

What do you see when you look at Jesus?

JG

MAUNDY THURSDAY

Spotlight on Sam 'As One Who Serves'

J. R. R. Tolkien, *The Lord of the Rings*

Tolkien has a special place in his books for those that serve, most especially Sam. Sam Gamgee is Frodo's gardener who finds himself drawn into the quest to destroy the Ring having overheard the plans through an open window. But, despite his humble status, he reveals himself to have heroic qualities in the manner in which he supports Frodo – at one point quite literally carrying his master on his back, as the two make their way to Mount Doom. His name is a shortened form of Samwise, which is derived from an Old English word meaning 'semi-wise', an equivalent of the modern English word 'halfwit'. But that name in no way defines him, since Sam shows considerable shrewdness in his unwillingness to trust Gollum. And yet, when presented with the opportunity to kill Gollum, he shows mercy, inspired in part by his own experience of the heavy burden imposed by carrying the Ring.

Although he is required to accompany Frodo to Rivendell, Sam subsequently refuses to be parted from his master. When Frodo tries to leave the Fellowship by boat, Sam pursues him, even jumping into the water despite being unable to swim. Following the Breaking of the Fellowship, Sam is the only one of the original group who continues to accompany Frodo on his dangerous quest. It is Sam who manages to overcome Shelob, the terrible spider, succeeding where even the doughtiest soldier of old Gondor or most savage Orc had failed.

Sam's first thought after the exhausting battle is for his master, who has been badly stung by the spider. Fearing that his master is dead, Sam despairs at the prospect of being parted from him: 'Frodo, Mr. Frodo! ... Don't leave me here alone! It's your Sam calling. Don't go where I can't follow!'[77] It is also Sam who recovers the Ring from Frodo before he is taken by the Orcs, bravely reasoning that, as the last of the company tasked with ensuring the errand does not fail, it is his job to ensure its success. Loath to put himself forward for a task for which he feels unsuited, Sam realizes that he hasn't put himself forward but rather has been put forward against his will.

It is Sam who tracks Frodo down to Cirith Ungol, where he is imprisoned, and manages to bring about his release. While Frodo is delighted to be reunited with his friend and rescued from the tower, he despairs for the loss of the Ring. Sam is able to restore the Ring, having safely guarded it while he journeyed to find Frodo, and thereby salvage the quest. But, in returning the Ring, Sam experiences a reluctance to hand it over – not because he wants its power for himself, but rather because of the burden he knows it places on his master. On learning that the Ring is safe, Frodo is initially overjoyed, but that delight quickly turns to suspicion and anger as the power of the Ring begins to work on Frodo. When Sam offers to share the burden of carrying the Ring, Frodo calls him a thief and refuses to countenance such an arrangement. This extreme possessiveness contrasts strongly with Sam's reluctance to take the Ring in the first place and his relief in returning it to its owner.

For Tolkien, Sam embodies the virtues of loyalty and bravery even when confronted with overwhelming opposition and hopelessness. The relationship between Frodo and Sam recalls that between an army officer and his batman, as experienced by Tolkien in World War One. As Tolkien himself admitted, although of lesser rank than himself, he recognized privates and batmen as the superior servicemen. Sam's bravery and loyalty extend to the very end of the quest. As Frodo's strength continues to weaken over the final journey to Mount Doom, Sam offers to share the burden of the Ring but again is vigorously rebuffed. Determined to lighten his master's load, Sam picks Frodo up and carries him up the mountain on his back, an image that recalls the way Simon of Cyrene helps carry Jesus' cross to Golgotha.

Through Sam's character, Tolkien shows even a lowly and humble figure can be courageous. While Sam may not have strength or noble blood, his loyalty towards his master and determination to help him, whatever the cost to himself, lead him to great acts of courage and heroism.

Reflection

Read Galatians 6.2:

> Bear one another's burdens, and in this way you will fulfil the law of Christ.

Do you need the courage to ask for support? Whose burdens can you help shoulder?

SH

GOOD FRIDAY

Tolkien, Lewis and the Road to the Cross

C. S. Lewis, *The Lion, the Witch and the Wardrobe*;
J. R. R. Tolkien, *The Return of the King*;
Anon., 'The Dream of the Rood'

The events of Good Friday are so seminal, so foundational for a Christian understanding of all the things the world fears, weakness, helplessness, defeat, death. Foundational because in Christ God enters into all of these from weakness and apparent defeat to death itself, and transforms them all so that his strength is made perfect in weakness and death is swallowed up in victory. That pattern and that transformation are central to the understanding of both Lewis and Tolkien so it is natural that we find that pattern in their writings, more explicitly in Lewis' account of Aslan's suffering and death on the Stone Table, more subtly in Tolkien's account of the last part of the journey to Mount Doom.

The scourging of Jesus and his mocking by the soldiers, the pseudo-homage of the purple robe and crown of thorns, all these become, in Lewis' 'supposal', in Aslan's passion, the binding with cruelly tight cords, the shaving of his beautiful mane, his dismissal as just a cat, the mocking of the tormentors, and so on. Lewis wisely does not show a mode of death that is to be a parallel with crucifixion but simply has the girls turn away at the last moment and leaves the reader to imagine what has been done to him.

Likewise Tolkien re-imagines, rather than simply reproduces, the elements of the Passion as he understood them. As a practising

Catholic, Tolkien would have been familiar with the Stations of the Cross, the 14 traditional stopping places on Christ's Via Dolorosa, his way of suffering. Three of these are about Jesus staggering and falling under the weight of the cross, and we can see an echo of these in the way that the Ring, Frodo's burden, grows heavier and heavier as he nears the Cracks of Doom. Another 'station of the cross' is the time when Simon of Cyrene carries Jesus' cross for a while, and as we have already seen, Sam Gamgee takes on that role when he carries Frodo himself. Another one of the stations, the tenth, is called 'Christ is stripped of his garments', and Tolkien would have learned to reflect on how this loosening, stripping away of outer possessions, was itself part of the *kenosis*, the self-emptying of Christ which begins at the incarnation. We see this at the point when Sam and Frodo cast off both the orc armour and, crucially, the precious cooking gear Sam has brought so far. This is not simply a practical lightening of the load, it is also a courageous admission that they don't think they'll be coming back, that the end of their journey will be self-sacrifice. In some ways, and paradoxically, the casting off of the useless weight of the armour is itself a kind of stripping for battle. Tolkien would have been familiar with the lines from the Anglo-Saxon poem 'The Dream of the Rood' in which the Passion is narrated by the cross itself, and the cross sees this stripping of Jesus not as an imposed humiliation but as a heroic preparation:

> Then the young Hero – it was God Almighty –
> Strong and steadfast, stripped himself for battle;
> He climbed up on the high gallows, constant in his purpose,
> Mounted it in the sight of many, mankind to ransom.[78]

One measure of how effective the re-imagining of these great themes has been is that when we ourselves return from these encounters in Narnia and Middle-earth to the actual accounts of the Passion in the Gospels and in Paul's letters, our response is deepened; the freely accepted sufferings of Aslan and Frodo have actually given us a more imaginatively enriched and informed response to the real events of Good Friday.

Reflection

Read Mark 15.16–39.

Meet these events afresh this Good Friday. Imagine being there – put yourself in the shoes of the onlookers, the soldiers, the thieves on the cross.

JG, MG, SH

HOLY SATURDAY

Pause, Poise and Turning Point

J. R. R. Tolkien, *The Return of the King*

One of the most dramatic moments in *The Lord of the Rings*, indeed the climax and turning point of the entire tale, comes as a kind of hush in all things, a strange stillness as the fate of the world hangs in the balance even as Frodo and Gollum struggle and teeter on the brink of Mount Doom. Indeed, even in the moment of deliverance when the Ring falls with Gollum to the fire, and Frodo, freed at last of his burden, falls forward, visible to Sam at last, there is a kind of pause, before the moment when Sauron's dark realm falls into ruin. Sam carries Frodo away from the edge: 'And there upon the dark threshold of the Sammath Naur high upon the plains of Mordor, such wonder and terror came on him that he stood still, forgetting all else, and gazed as one turned to stone.'[79]

This same moment of pause, this same sense of being on a threshold, poised and waiting for a turning point, comes upon the Captains of the West, gathered at the black gates of Mordor. They have defied 'the mouth of Sauron', the dark Lord's emissary, and are about to enter into battle against impossible odds – indeed battle has started – when a change comes. Sauron has suddenly become aware that the Ring itself has been taken to Mount Doom and is within a hairsbreadth of destruction. At last he sees, what he never could have guessed, that Elves and Men have chosen weakness, self-emptying, *kenosis*, have chosen to let go of the Ring and destroy it rather than conquer through it. His whole will is bent towards the Cracks of Doom and the struggle there and so his army totters, bereft of leadership. The Captains of the West are about to charge when 'Gandalf lifted up his arms and called once more in a clear voice: "Stand, Men of the West! Stand and wait! This is the hour of doom."' And then, after this hushed moment, the tide turns, the darkness breaks, the works of Sauron start to fall asunder, the 'Black Gate is hurled in ruin' and Gandalf declares, 'The Realm of Sauron has ended, the ring-bearer has fulfilled his Quest.'[80]

Tolkien is very careful to tell us that all this happens on 25 March, a date that was once of huge significance to all of Christendom and was still immensely significant to Tolkien. The early church Fathers believed that 25 March had been the date of the crucifixion, and since that was one of the two great turning points in the story of salvation, they surmised that the other turning point, Mary's 'yes' to the Angel Gabriel at the annunciation, the moment when Christ began his human life in her womb, must also have been 25 March. Indeed veneration for this date, so significant in our salvation, led people to believe that it was also the date of the first day of creation!

We may not be so confident about the exact dates in calendars, but we can all feel, as we come to the pause and poise of Holy Saturday, the day of expectant stillness between the apparent calamity of Good Friday, and the glorious renewal, the beginning of the new creation on Easter Day, that we are at a hushed turning point. We have, as Frodo says to Sam, 'come to the end of all things' on Good Friday, and now on this Holy Saturday we begin to dare to hope that that End is also the threshold of a Beginning which will dawn on Easter Sunday. For medieval Christians Holy Saturday is indeed the day when the dark tower falls, when 'the Black Gate was hurled in ruin'. For it was on Holy Saturday that Jesus descended into hell and overthrew Satan's kingdom, setting free the prisoners. This is why Orthodox icons of the Resurrection show Jesus standing on the broken gates of hell and holding Adam and Eve by the hand, rescued from ruin, just as Frodo and Sam are lifted out of the ruin of Mount Doom, on the wings of eagles.

Reflection

Read John 19.38–42.

Tolkien dated the destruction of the Ring to 25 March, the date of the crucifixion. What parallels do you discern between Frodo and Sam's journey into Mordor and Christ's journey towards the cross?

MG

EASTER SUNDAY

Resurrection of Aslan and the Field of Cormallen

C. S. Lewis, *The Lion, the Witch and the Wardrobe*;
J. R. R. Tolkien, *The Return of the King*

It is the two girls, Susan and Lucy, who remain with Aslan following his death, mourning his loss, trying to remove the muzzle and loosen the ropes that bind him. Here, the narrator addresses the reader directly, poignantly capturing the sense of desperation and sorrow the two sisters experienced: 'I hope no one who reads this book has been quite as miserable as Susan and Lucy were that night.'[81] The girls' loving concern for Aslan is rewarded when Lucy and Susan are the first to witness his resurrection, Susan feeling the warmth of his breath when Aslan licks her forehead. The scene draws on the biblical stories of the resurrection, with Aslan's breathing on the girls recalling Jesus' breathing on his disciples in John 20. But where Jesus tells Mary Magdalen not to touch him, Aslan challenges the sisters to do exactly that, engaging them in the children's game of 'catch me if you can'. The whole scene shifts from one of despair and sorrow to one of innocent joy, with the children's game recalling that of hide-and-seek with which the story began.

Frodo and Sam experience similar feelings of despair following the destruction of Mount Doom, with Frodo renouncing all hope of survival. And yet, just at this moment of desperation, they are swept away by eagles and taken to Ithilien, where they are able to recover in comfort. Having awoken, the Hobbits are then led to a reception on the Field of Cormallen in their honour, where crowds cheer their names and sing their praise. Despite their ragged hobbit clothing, Frodo and Sam are welcomed by Aragorn, placed on a throne and invited to a great feast. As noted yesterday, the Easter context of this scene is made explicit by Tolkien by giving the date of Sauron's fall as 25 March. Frodo and Sam rise again on 8 April, with Sam rejoicing in feeling like 'spring after winter, and sun on the leaves',[82] recalling the coming of spring with Aslan's return to Narnia. It is a passage that moved its author to shed tears that blotted the pages on which he wrote, as he recalled in a letter to his aunt, Jane Neave.[83]

We've already met the term eucatastrophe, coined by Tolkien to refer to an unexpected fortunate turn of events, a 'sudden and miraculous grace', which, while it does not deny the existence of its opposite, dyscatastrophe, sorrow and failure, does deny universal final defeat. In such moments, Tolkien says, this sudden turn gives the reader a 'piercing glimpse of joy, and heart's desire, that for a moment passes outside the frame, rends indeed the very web of story, and lets a gleam come through'. We see this contrast clearly in *The Lion, the Witch and the Wardrobe*, where the promise of the happy ending, with Aslan's return and his defeat of the White Witch, is suddenly and cruelly denied by the Witch invoking her right to kill Edmund the traitor, leading to Aslan's self-sacrifice in his place.

But, of course, this is not the end of the story. The eucatastrophe is still to come. Aslan rises from the dead, the stone statues are restored to life, the Witch's reign is over and the children are installed as kings and queens of Narnia, sitting on the thrones at Cair Paravel. Aslan is able to defeat death because, when a willing victim who has committed no treachery is killed in a traitor's stead, the Stone Table cracks and Death itself begins to work backwards, undoing all the harm that the Witch had caused. Sam hopes for a similar redeeming of the past when he awakes and realizes that neither he nor Frodo has died, asking Gandalf if their victory over Sauron means that everything sad is going to come untrue.

Both writers are exploiting the fairy-tale convention of the happy ending to present the greatest of all eucatastrophes: one in which story and History meet, the web of story is torn and a splinter of light, or what Lewis would call a stab of Joy, breaks through. As Tolkien concludes in the essay 'On Fairy-Stories':

> There is no tale ever told that men would rather find was true, and none which so many sceptical men have accepted as true on its own merits. For the Art of it has the supremely convincing tone of Primary Art, that is, of Creation. To reject it leads either to sadness or to wrath.[84]

Reflection

Read Luke 24.1–53.

What is your response to this story? Are you like the women who believe and rush off to tell others, or like the others who dismiss their story as nonsense? As you reflect on this passage on Easter Sunday, consider what areas of your heart may be being illuminated by the splinters of light it gives out.

JG, MG, SH

Acknowledgements

This book began as a Lent course run at St Andrew's Church, Linton Road, Oxford, a few doors down from the house, 20 Northmoor Road, where Tolkien lived when he wrote his most famous books. Revd Paul White put Julia and Simon together to go on this journey so he must be acknowledged as the original Elrond to the project. Thank you, Paul.

We'd also like to thank the congregation of St Andrew's for their input – they were our Uncle Andrew guinea pigs to be sent out to the Wood between the Worlds. We then repeated the course a year later at St Michael's parish church, Blewbury, a village near Oxford which is very like the ones that inspired Hobbiton. So thank you to all the Hobbits/people of the village who participated.

Malcolm joined the fellowship after that – like Gandalf he turned up a little late but also perfectly on time – and we three have enjoyed going on this pilgrimage together to see Lent through with the Inklings. Thank you to all our readers for coming along with us.

Thanks to Parker Williams for allowing us to use his photo of the gates of Addison's Walk. All other photos belong to Julia Golding.

Further Up, and Further In

If you are looking for more reading on the Inklings, or want to follow up books we mention, you might like to dip into the following books:

Owen Barfield, 1967, *History in English Words*, Grand Rapids, MI: Eerdman.

Humphrey Carpenter, 1978, *The Inklings: C. S. Lewis, J. R. R. Tolkien, Charles Williams and Their Friends*, George Allen and Unwin.

Colin Duriez, 2005, *J. R. R. Tolkien and C. S. Lewis: The Story of their Friendship*, Stroud: Sutton Publishing.

Colin Duriez, 2015, *The Oxford Inklings: Lewis, Tolkien and Their Circle*, Oxford: Lion Books.

Diana Glyer, 2015, *Bandersnatch: C. S. Lewis, J. R. R. Tolkien, and the Creative Collaboration of the Inklings*, Kent, OH: Kent State University Press.

Malcolm Guite, 2021, *David's Crown: Sounding the Psalms*, London: Canterbury Press.

Simon Horobin, 2024, *C. S. Lewis's Oxford*, Oxford: Bodleian Library Publishing.

Grevel Lindop, 2015, *Charles Williams: The Third Inkling*, Oxford: Oxford University Press.

Harry L. Poe and J. Veneman, 2009, *The Inklings of Oxford: C. S. Lewis, J. R. R. Tolkien, and Their Friends*, Grand Rapids, MI: Zondervan.

Michael Ward, 2008, *Planet Narnia: The Seven Heavens in the Imagination of C. S. Lewis*, Oxford: Oxford University Press.

Philip Zaleski and Carol Zaleski, 2015, *The Fellowship: The Literary Lives of the Inklings*, New York: Farrar, Straus and Giroux.

The following are readily available paperback editions of some of the better-known works discussed in this book:

Works by C. S. Lewis

The Cosmic Trilogy (also known as The Ransom Trilogy; 3 vols beginning with *Out of the Silent Planet*), 2005, London: HarperCollins.
The Chronicles of Narnia (7 vols beginning with *The Lion, the Witch and the Wardrobe*), 2012, London: HarperCollins.
The Great Divorce, 2012, London: William Collins.
The Screwtape Letters, 2012, London: William Collins.
Surprised by Joy, 2012, London: William Collins.

Works by J. R. R. Tolkien

The Lord of the Rings (3 vols in 1), 2005, London: HarperCollins.
The Hobbit, 2011, London: HarperCollins.
The Silmarillion, 2013, London: HarperCollins.

Other editions are available and readers may well have their own; we therefore cite these works by chapter rather than page number in the endnotes that follow. Full references for other works are given in the notes.

Endnotes

1. C. S. Lewis, *The Lion, the Witch and the Wardrobe*, Ch. 5.
2. J. R. R. Tolkien, *The Fellowship of the Ring*, Book II, Ch. 7.
3. C. S. Lewis, *The Voyage of the 'Dawn Treader'*, Ch. 6.
4. Douglas Adams, 2002, *The Hitchhiker's Guide to the Galaxy: A Trilogy in Four Parts*, London: Picador, p. 70.
5. C. S. Lewis, 2012, *The Discarded Image*, Cambridge: Cambridge University Press, pp. 99–100.
6. Lewis, *The Discarded Image*, p. 12.
7. Lewis, *The Discarded Image*, p. 218.
8. Lewis, *The Discarded Image*, p. 223.
9. Lewis, *The Discarded Image*, p. 222.
10. C. S. Lewis, *Out of the Silent Planet*, Ch. 5.
11. C. S. Lewis, 1939, *Rehabilitations and Other Essays*, Oxford: Oxford University Press, p. 157.
12. J. R. R. Tolkien, *The Return of the King*, Book VI, Ch. 2.
13. Canto 34, lines 133–9 in Dante, *Inferno*, translated by Robin Kirkpatrick, Penguin Classics, 2006, pp. 311–12.
14. Shakespeare, *The Merchant of Venice*, Act V Scene 1, lines 58–65.
15. C. S. Lewis, *The Magician's Nephew*, Ch. 8.
16. Lewis, *The Voyage of the 'Dawn Treader'*, Ch. 14.
17. Lewis, *Out of the Silent Planet*, Ch. 5.
18. J. R. R. Tolkien, 2024, *Collected Poems*, eds. Christina Skull and Wayne D. Hammond, London: HarperCollins, No. 136.
19. Lewis Carroll, 2001, *The Annotated Alice*, ed. Martin Gardner, London: Penguin, p. 11.
20. Tolkien, *The Fellowship of the Ring*, Book II, Ch. 9.
21. J. R. R. Tolkien, *The Two Towers*, Book III, Ch. 8.
22. Tolkien, *The Two Towers*, Book III, Ch. 4.
23. Tolkien, *The Fellowship of the Ring*, Book II, Ch. 2.
24. Humphrey Carpenter and Christopher Tolkien (eds), 2023, *The Letters of J. R. R. Tolkien*, London: HarperCollins, Letter 154, p. 293.
25. C. S. Lewis, *Prince Caspian*, Ch. 5.

26 Tolkien, *The Return of the King*, Book VI, Ch. 1.
27 Charles Williams, 1932, *The Greater Trumps*, London: Victor Gollancz, p. 141.
28 T. S. Eliot, 'Burnt Norton', part II, lines 16–17.
29 Lewis, *The Lion, the Witch and the Wardrobe*, Ch. 3.
30 Tolkien, *The Fellowship of the Ring*, Book I, Ch. 2.
31 'The Battle of Maldon' in J. R. R. Tolkien, 2003, *The Battle of Maldon together with The Homecoming of Beorhtnoth*, ed. Peter Grybauskas, London: HarperCollins, p. 67.
32 Tolkien, *The Return of the King*, Book V, Ch. 4.
33 Tolkien, *The Fellowship of the Ring*, Book II, Ch. 2.
34 Shakespeare, *A Midsummer Night's Dream*, Act V Scene 1, lines 14–17.
35 C. S. Lewis, *Surprised by Joy*, Ch. XI.
36 Both works can be found in J. R. R. Tolkien, 2001, *Tree and Leaf: including the poem Mythopoeia*, ed. Christopher Tolkien, London: HarperCollins.
37 C. S. Lewis, 1982, *Of This and Other Worlds*, ed. Walter Hooper, London: William Collins, p. 78.
38 Lewis, *Of This and Other Worlds*, p. 79.
39 Lewis, *The Magician's Nephew*, Ch. 9.
40 Colin Duriez, 2021, *Dorothy L. Sayers: A Biography*, Oxford: Lion Books, p. 11.
41 Dorothy L. Sayers, 1979, *The Mind of the Maker*, London: Harper & Row, p. 29.
42 Sayers, *The Mind of the Maker*, p. 67.
43 Carpenter and Tolkien, *The Letters of J. R. R. Tolkien*, p. 119.
44 C. S. Lewis, 1942, *A Preface to Paradise Lost*, Oxford: Oxford University Press, p. 47.
45 Lewis, *Surprised by Joy*, Ch. IX.
46 Humphrey Carpenter, 1978, *The Inklings*, London: George Allen and Unwin, p. 43.
47 See note 36.
48 C. S. Lewis, *The Screwtape Letters*, Letter 24.
49 J. R. R. Tolkien, *The Hobbit*, Ch. XVIII.
50 Tolkien, *The Two Towers*, Book IV, Ch. 8.
51 Carpenter and Tolkien, *The Letters of J. R. R. Tolkien*, p. 246.
52 Quoted in Colin Duriez, 2015, *The Oxford Inklings: Lewis, Tolkien and Their Circle*, Oxford: Lion Books, p. 219.
53 Lewis, *The Voyage of the 'Dawn Treader'*, Ch. 16.
54 Carpenter and Tolkien, *The Letters of J. R. R. Tolkien*, p. 103.
55 J. R. R. Tolkien, 2015, *The Lays of Beleriand*, ed. Christopher Tolkien, London: HarperCollins, p. 151.

56 Walter Hooper (ed.), 2004–07, *The Collected Letters of C. S. Lewis*, 3 vols, San Francisco: HarperCollins, vol. II, p. 991.
57 Carpenter and Tolkien, *The Letters of J. R. R. Tolkien*, p. 362.
58 https://george-macdonald.com/resources/chesterton_introduction.html
59 George MacDonald, 1998, *The Princess and the Goblin*, New York: ACC Children's Classics, pp. 13–14.
60 MacDonald, *The Princess and the Goblin*, pp. 72–3.
61 MacDonald, *The Princess and the Goblin*, p. 74.
62 Hooper, *The Collected Letters of C. S. Lewis*, vol. III, p. 480.
63 Hooper, *The Collected Letters of C. S. Lewis*, vol. III, p. 971.
64 Ray Bradbury, 2015, *Zen in the Art of Writing*, London: HarperCollins, p. 114.
65 J. R. R. Tolkien, 2021, *The Nature of Middle-earth*, ed. Carl F. Hofstetter, London: HarperCollins, p. 230.
66 Carpenter and Tolkien, *The Letters of J. R. R. Tolkien*, pp. 83 and 66.
67 Owen Barfield, 1967, *History in English Words*, Grand Rapids, MI: Eerdman, p. 17.
68 Barfield, *History in English Words*, p. 143.
69 C. S. Lewis, *The Silver Chair*, Ch. 12.
70 Lewis, *Surprised by Joy*, Ch. XI.
71 C. S. Lewis, *Perelandra*, Ch. 11.
72 Lewis, *The Magician's Nephew*, Ch. 12.
73 Tolkien, *The Two Towers*, Book III, Ch. 5.
74 C. S. Lewis, 1978, *Till We Have Faces*, London: HarperCollins, p. 124.
75 C. S. Lewis, *The Last Battle*, Ch. 13.
76 Lewis, *Till We Have Faces*, p. 308.
77 Tolkien, *The Two Towers*, Book IV, Ch. 10.
78 Lines 34–42 in Helen Gardner, 1970, *The Dream of the Rood: An Exercise in Verse Translation*, London: Constable.
79 Tolkien, *The Return of the King*, Book VI, Ch. 3.
80 Tolkien, *The Return of the King*, Book VI, Ch. 4.
81 Lewis, *The Lion, the Witch and the Wardrobe*, Ch. 15.
82 Tolkien, *The Return of the King*, Book VI, Ch. 4.
83 Carpenter and Tolkien, *The Letters of J. R. R. Tolkien*, p. 454.
84 Tolkien, *Tree and Leaf: including the poem Mythopoeia*, p. 72.

www.ingramcontent.com/pod-product-compliance
Lightning Source LLC
Chambersburg PA
CBHW020533080526
44583CB00013B/844